# REAL ALES
## for the home brewer

# REAL ALES
## for the home brewer

Marc Ollosson

Amateur Winemaker Books

Dedicated to Neil Barry Haughey, Duncan Hook and
Jean-Pierre Vossen whose support and friendship made it all
possible.

Special Interest Model Books Ltd
P.O.Box 327
Poole, Dorset BH15 2RG
England

www.specialinterestbooks.co.uk

First published 1997 by Nexus Special Interests

This second edition published 2014 by
Amateur Winemaker Books, an imprint of
Special Interest Model Books Ltd

© Marc Ollosson 1997 and 2014

ISBN 978 185486 269 3

Printed and bound in Malta by Melita Press

# Contents

**Belhaven Brewery Co.:** *70/-, 60/-, Sandy Hunter's Traditional Ale,
80/-,St Andrews Ale, Belhaven 90/-*

**Borve Brew House:** *Borve Ale, Tall Ships India Pale Ale,
Aberdeen Union Street 200*

**Harviestoun Brewery:** *Waverley 70/-, Original80/-,
Montrose Ale, Ptarmigan, Schiehallion, Old Manor*

**Maclay & Co.:** *Maclay 70/-, Broadsword,
Kane's Amber Ale, Maclay Scotch Ale*

**Orkney Brewery:** *Raven Ale, Dragonhead Stout, Dark Island, Skullsplitter*

**Tomintoul Brewery :** *Tomintoul Wild Cat, Tomintoul Stag, Tomintoul 80/-*

**Castle Eden Brewery:** *Castle Eden Ale, Whitbread Porter, Winter Royal*

**Malton Brewery Co.:** *Malton Pale Ale, Double Chance Bitter,
Pickwick's Porter, Owd Bob*

**Marston Moor Brewery:** *Cromwell Bitter, Brewers Pride, Porter*

6

# Introduction

Ever since I had my first pint of beer, at a younger age than the law would allow, I've been intrigued as to how it was made and why each one tasted so different using just four basic ingredients; malt, hops, yeast and water. It was only when I found out that there were over 20 different malt grains, over 30 different hop varieties, numerous adjuncts and that each brewery had its own strain of yeast that I began to appreciate why each beer is unique.

This led me to a great pastime – brewing. My aim, then, was to brew a beer like I was drinking in the pub.

Like the majority of brewers I started with a 1.5kg kit, and while the brew was enjoyable it still lacked something. Other brands followed as did different kit sizes, 1.8kg and 3kg. Glenbrew, Ironmaster and Muntons soon became firm favourites, their beers were full flavoured with consistent quality. Experimenting with a kit seemed a good idea, but how to go about it and what to use was a mystery. Brewing Products Ltd. solved the problem by providing recipes with their Telford's and Ironmaster kits which allow you to brew different styles of beer using various ingredients and one of their kits as a base. With a horde of thirsty friends and family there was never a shortage of guinea pigs to test the latest brew on.

It is a shame that all manufacturers don't give a few recipes with their kits. Unfortunately they seem to forget that there is a middle ground where brewers want to stop using a standard kit, but do not wish to progress to brewing from scratch. Before long the frustration of not being able to brew with the full range of ingredients got the better of me. My boiler shared my feelings and decided to show its displeasure by packing up as soon as the next brew came to the boil!

Two years after starting the hobby, armed with Thorne's combined mash bin/ boiler, a grain bag and a copy of Dave Line's *Brewing Beers Like Those You Buy* (published by Amateur Winemaker Books), the aim of producing a home-brew copy of a commercial beer was finally achieved. Some mashers might ask "What took you so long?". My answer would have to be "Why rush a good thing?". Apart from a few mistakes, boil overs and smashed hydrometers and thermometers, I thoroughly enjoyed the kits, the experiments and the extract recipes.

Kits are only the first rung on the brewing ladder. How far up you go depends entirely on how much quality and flexibility you want, but if you started brewing because you enjoy beer, then you owe it to yourself, your tastebuds and your barrel to keep moving.

There's no need to scramble up ... just relax and enjoy the beers brewed along the way.

# About this book

Perhaps the greatest event in a drinker's life was the advent of the lorry and the motorway – or was it the train and railway? Anyway, all of a sudden beers brewed in the farthest reaches of the land could be enjoyed in the comfort of the local pub.

In the bleak and dismal years prior to these momentous inventions, drinkers in South Wales had become accustomed to the local brew. Tales of the potency of S.A. Bitter were handed down from father to son, while they toiled hard in the pits. Other breweries, realising South Wales had been deprived of choice for generations, rushed to the region with hand pumps ready only to find out the sad truth – that drinkers had become 'Brains' washed and, even more depressing, landlords were the worst cases!

Today, many landlords and the brewery still try to convert drinkers with the slogan "It's Brains you want", S.A. Bitter is still talked about and devoted followers have christened it 'Skull Attack', although perhaps this name was born of fond memories, as at 4.2% the potency seems to have been lost in the misty and song-filled valleys of time.

While this is written with tongue firmly in cheek, other beer-loving brewers must have felt the same way, because by the time our shop in Bridgend opened, many of them had ploughed through Dave Line's *Brewing Beers Like Those You Buy* and were in search of more recipes.

Lack of recipes continued to be a problem, until someone suggested that I put those years in college to good use and write a computer program to produce recipes from available information. Although the program was still in use at the shop, tailoring recipes to brewers' individual requirements, the thought of a book had all but disappeared. What I hadn't counted on was the dedication of one customer and good friend, Ivor White, who mashed his way through an incredible number of available recipes, so after three years, this book finally came to see the light of day, and although some recipes may have appeared in print before, they have all been recalculated to take into account any changes made to the recipe.

These recipes *can only attempt* to copy a particular ale, due to the different variables in the brewing process, especially the yeast strain, which probably has the most influence on a brew. An exact copy would be very difficult to brew at home. The recipes are mainly formulated for mashing, using grain, but all can be brewed with a partial mash using a diastatic malt extract and some recipes can be brewed with an unhopped light-coloured non-diastatic malt extract.

A light malt extract is specified because the malt grains should provide all the necessary colour, as is the case with full mashes. However, to complicate matters, the depth of colour in the extract can vary from manufacturer to manufacturer, although Muntons do give their malts an official EBC colour rating. So if your brew is paler than expected then try a medium extract next time or a different brand of malt.

Although at the time of writing all malt grains and hop varieties listed in the recipes are available to home brewers, your specialist shop may not stock them, but your friendly retailer is a wealth of information and should be able to suggest alternatives.

It would be impossible to list the names of all the people who have made this book possible, mainly because I don't know yours! You, the home brewer, deserve the majority of thanks. It is your dedication and interest in a truly rewarding hobby that has put this book on the shelves.

I would also like to thank Richard Wheeler of Tuckers Maltings (Newton Abbot) for providing the technical data required for the malts and for reminding me about mash efficiencies. Tuckers has a great visitors centre which explains and shows the entire malting process.

It is also worth pointing out that many breweries will gladly and proudly show you how their beers are made. So if you're interested in the commercial version of one of the recipes in this book then why not contact the brewery and see if they offer guided tours?

Calculating hop weights is so much easier when you've got accurate alpha acid levels to work with. Many thanks to Brupaks for providing these figures and actually printing them on their packaging! They also provided the malt and hop descriptions.

I'm indebted to the commercial breweries; their increasing openness about their recipes and ingredients has taken home brewing along a few stages and provided me with a great deal of enjoyment, both at home and down the pub.

*Cheers!*

# Equipment

Quality beers can be brewed with the most basic of equipment, so possessing a full armoury of equipment doesn't necessarily mean you will produce vastly superior beers, but it does mean that you will be able to produce quality beers with greater ease.

The following equipment is essential to brew the recipes in this book:

- 25 litre fermenting bin with lid

- Thermometer

- Hydrometer and jar

- Weighing scales (preferably electronic, for greater accuracy)

- Mash tun (for all grain brewers)

- Large boiler

- Pressure barrel, mini kegs or bottles.

You **should always check and mark** the 23 litre level on your fermenting bin – the calibrations printed on them are, at best, for guidance only.

Thermometers should occasionally be checked for their accuracy. Bring a pan of water to the boil and dip your thermometer in. A reading of 100°C should be seen, if not make a note of the difference and remember to adjust by this amount every time. Electronic thermometers, while available and extremely accurate, are expensive.

Hydrometers are only accurate at 20°C – any variance to this temperature will affect the gravity readings that you take. Refer to your hydrometer instructions for correction figures.

Hambleton Bard manufacture a thermo-hydrometer which combines both a thermometer and hydrometer and comes with a correction scale printed on the unit itself and full instructions. You will also need a matching trial jar as the thermo-hydrometer is longer than a standard hydrometer. Note: as the thermometer scale only goes up to 30°C, do not dip the instrument in boiling water, but check it with another thermometer.

Burco boilers can be purchased second hand. Thorne Electrim and Ritchie Products manufacture purpose-built boilers for home brewers. Brupaks can supply hop strainers which eliminate the need for bailing the wort or a separate hop back.

Mash tuns can either be home-made or purchased new. The Thorne and Ritchie boilers are supplied with accurate thermostats which allow them to be used for the purpose of mashing.

There are various pressure barrels available; if you can only store your keg on the floor, then a barrel with its tap mid-way up the body may be more suitable.

Mini kegs are 4.5l stainless steel cans; because of their size they are easily portable and can be placed in the fridge to cool your beer down. If you are using pressure barrels or mini kegs, then there will come a time when you have to inject $CO_2$ into your beer. The most economical gas systems are those which use the large gas cylinders as opposed to the small 8g bulbs.

Hambleton Bard and Widget World supply large size cylinders for the home brewer. The Widget system does offer several benefits, such as increased safety, adaptability and the option to change the cylinder for a nitrogen mix (this should prove to be of interest to stout and caffrey-type ales fans)

A partnership development between Weltonhurst and Widget has resulted in the Connoisseurs barrel. This barrel has a built-in pressure gauge and comes with a chrome plated tap unit that is fitted to the cap.

Although beer bottles can be obtained from many sources, it is essential that they are free of defects and be capable of withstanding the pressures that build up during secondary fermentation. Unless you are using swing-stopper type bottles, like those used for *Grolsch*, then you will need crown caps and a suitable capper

# Malt extract, sugars, syrups, malt grains, unmalted grains and adjuncts, Irish moss

## Malt extract

At one time or another all of us have probably brewed with this ingredient. It is produced by mashing malted barley and then concentrating the wort into a thick syrup. The syrup is then either tinned or subjected to a further process, known as spray drying, to produce spray dried malt extract.

There are two major types of extract available: diastatic and non-diastatic.

### Diastatic malt

Because this extract is concentrated at lower temperatures it still retains the diastatic enzymes required to convert starches, in grains and adjuncts, into fermentable sugars. Brewing Products, John Bull and Edme all produce a diastatic malt extract.

Although a short mash is required, this malt does allow the brewer to use the full range of brewing ingredients available.

NB. Brewing Products market their diastatic malt as DME, and it is an excellent malt to brew with. Edme's DMS is also quite good but I cannot comment on John Bull as I haven't tried it.

### Non-diastatic malt

This extract allows the brewer to avoid the mash process. Unfortunately only grains which do not require starch to sugar conversion can be used, these being:

- Crystal malt
- Chocolate malt
- Black malt
- Roasted barley
- Carapils

This extract saves the brewer time in the brewing process but at the expense of the amount of ingredients, therefore limiting the number of recipes available.

## Sugars

Believe it or not, household sugar isn't fermentable straight away. First the yeast has to produce an enzyme (invertase) to break it down into glucose and fructose. Because of this, breweries tend not to use household white cane or beet sugar, instead they use invert sugar. This form of sugar has already been broken down into glucose and fructose, which saves the yeast doing the job. Cane and beet sugar are interchangeable.

Where a recipe calls for invert sugar you can use household white granulated sugar instead, or you could hang the expense and use golden syrup, which is liquid invert sugar.

15

## Syrups

Maltose and glucose syrups are not 100% fermentable, and as such they won't thin out the body of the beer as much as household white sugar (try using them in your favourite kit and taste the difference!). Where a recipe calls for maltose syrup you can substitute with glucose syrup and vice versa.

I am unaware of any wholesaler selling these syrups (Edme and Ritchie market a 'liquid brewing sugar' but this contains barley syrup and is only recommended for kits), but check availability with your home-brew shop. If you still encounter difficulty in getting hold of these or you don't have a home-brew outlet close by, then try your local health food store – you should find glucose syrup on their shelves.

Barley syrup is made by mashing raw (unmalted) barley and throwing in a good dose of industrial enzymes. By bypassing the maltster, breweries can save quite a bit of money. This ingredient has found its way into some home-brew kits. Unfortunately, while it is far cheaper for manufacturers to use, they certainly don't pass these savings on and still charge you as if they were using 100% malt extract in their kits! Apart from increasing profits, I can't see why this industry needs to use barley syrup, except for brewing some of Dave Line's recipes, as no self-respecting commercial brewer uses or admits to using it. After all, the whole concept of home brewing is to produce commercial-quality real ales at home. The only way to do that is to use commercial-quality ingredients and not ingredients which commercial brewers shy away from.

## Malt grains

Obviously something like grain descriptions and colour ratings (EBC) can vary from maltster to maltster and wholesaler to wholesaler, but these should serve you as a good guide. Even the name of malt grains can vary between maltsters. For example, Maclay & Co. use Caramalt in their grist, but Tuckers Maltings (Newton Abbot) have called this malt Carapils (I believe just before printing they are changing its name back to Caramalt). Hence Carapils being listed as an ingredient in Broadsword & Maclay Scotch Ale.

**WHEAT MALT** (3–4 EBC) – normally used in conjunction with either pale or lager malts to produce wheat beers, but when used in small amounts in British ales it imparts a unique flavour and aids head retention.

**PALE MALT** (5 EBC) – provides the bulk of fermentable sugars in British beers. To retain a light colour it is kilned very dry between 95°C and 105°C. The three major varieties are Maris Otter, Pipkin and Halcyon.

**MILD ALE MALT** (6 EBC) – produced from Triumph barley. This malt is kilned slightly hotter than pale malt to give a fuller flavour.

**AMBER MALT** (90–110 EBC) – the grain is dried to 3% of its moisture content and then quickly heated to above 95°C. It is then kilned at around 140°C until the desired colour is reached. It gives a biscuit-type flavour and a golden colour.

**CRYSTAL MALT** (80–140 EBC) – the grains are dried between 65°C and 80°C which enables them to mash themselves and caramelise the resulting sugars. The grains are then kilned at 250°C until the desired colour is reached. Unsurpassed for adding a subtle sweetness to balance the hops.

**CARAPILS** (3–5 EBC) – like crystal malt, the sugar in the grain is allowed to caramelise, but it is not kilned at so high a temperature. This means it is very pale in colour. Carapils helps promote head formation and retention and gives the beer a fuller rounder flavour.

**BROWN MALT** (120–150 EBC) – modern brown malt is no longer smoked, but is amber kilned for a longer period to achieve a darker colour.

**CHOCOLATE MALT** (1000 EBC) – a highly roasted malt which, when used in small amounts, imparts a rich chocolatey flavour to beers such as porters and brown ales. Chocolate malt can also be used to darken bitters, although care should be taken over quantities used. A paler chocolate malt is also available at around 800 EBC, similar flavour but lighter in colour.

**BLACK MALT** (1200–1500 EBC) – highly kilned malt. Can be used to darken all ales, especially stouts, porters and many mild ales. Like chocolate malt, care should be taken over the quantities used.

## Unmalted grains and adjuncts

Most unmalted adjuncts are best used in flaked form. The flakes are produced first by cooking the raw grains in water, until the starches have gelatinised. They are then dried and passed through rollers to flatten them. The starches can then easily be converted into fermentable sugars by the enzymes in the malt.

**ROASTED BARLEY** – this is raw barley which has been roasted for as long as possible to make the darkest of all grains. It is rich in substances which aid the formation of a solid head. Its slightly burnt, bitter taste is best suited to the darker ales, especially stout. Roasted barley can also be used sparingly to darken other beers or to add some complexity to an ale.

17

**FLAKED BARLEY** – a versatile adjunct, particularly in stouts. It imparts a lovely grainy flavour, and although it can be used in quite large amounts in the darker beers it can cause hazes in the paler styles. Aids head retention and formation.

**TORRIFIED WHEAT** – this 'exploded' grain is used extensively to promote the head retention in bitters.

**FLAKED MAIZE** – derived from corn kernels, this cereal adds a delicate corn taste to beers. It is also beneficial to the clearing process, due to its low nitrogen content.

**WHEAT FLOUR** – its main purpose is to aid head retention, however many commercial breweries have now switched to using Torrified wheat.

Brupaks also market a full range of 'speciality' malt grains, for those brewers who like the quality German beers such as Kolsch, Alt and Dortmunder. Both smoked malt and roasted rye malt are available and these superb malts allow you to brew the classic Rauch and Roggen beers.

## Irish moss

This is dried seaweed. During the boil the Irish moss causes proteins and other solids to join together, which helps them to drop out once the boil is complete.

# Hop varieties

On a weight for weight basis, hops are probably the most expensive ingredient that you can put into your beer. Therefore it stands to reason that you should always brew with the best quality available to you.

For hundreds of years now hops have been used as the 'seasoning' in beer. Originally a wild-growing weed, the hop, a member of the cannabis family of plants, is now intensively cultivated. Its inherent poor resistance to disease and its low tolerance of adverse weather conditions have led to the development of many new varieties, which have been bred to combat disease while retaining flavour and bittering power.

Hops are used for three separate purposes, besides their preservative properties. First, they provide beer with bitterness. To obtain the maximum bitterness hops must be boiled in the wort for at least 1 hour, as the alpha acids are insoluble until they have been isomerised by the long boil. Unfortunately all of the aroma, and most of the flavour, is driven off along with the steam and it is common practice, therefore, to add hops to the boil in stages. The copper hops are introduced at the beginning of the boil. These will usually be rich in alpha acids with their flavouring properties less important.

Secondly, they provide beer with flavour. These hops are added late in the boil to preserve as much flavour as possible, with further additions to obtain a delicate bouquet.

Thirdly, they are used for 'dry hopping' – steeping raw hops in the finished beer – which is another widely used method of achieving a bouquet. These hops must always be as fresh as possible and of the finest quality.

Unfortunately, many recipes available have been formulated without regard for the alpha acid content of the hops and do not advise 'late hopping'. This can result in unbalanced beers with precious little hop flavour and aroma, which can be disappointing, especially for the novice brewer who will probably think it is he and not the recipe at fault.

Trying to copy the hop characteristics of a beer is probably the hardest task to face a home brewer. The commercial breweries constantly change the hop rates and proportions of varieties to maintain a consistent bitterness and hop flavour in the beer. They may only add a small proportion of late hops or they may add a large amount of dry hops (those dropped directly into the cask), but even varying these amounts slightly can add a whole new dimension to the flavour and aroma of the beer.

Hops tend to fall into three categories: bittering, aroma and dual purpose.

## Bittering hops

These are usually those with the highest alpha acid content. Alpha acid is the hop's bittering power, so hops with a high acid level are the most economical to use. However, there is a downside. Bittering hops can have a harsh taste and very little aroma therefore many breweries either use a blend of hops in the copper (boiler) or add quality aroma hops at the end of the boil (late hops) and/or directly to the cask.

**TARGET** – probably the most widely used high alpha acid hop, should only be used sparingly in the copper. Its flavour and aroma can be overpowering if used as a late hop.

**YEOMAN** – a high alpha acid hop, can be used to replace Northdown when unavailable, but it is unsuitable as a late hop and is best blended with other varieties.

**NORTHERN BREWER** – originally from Britain and now grown only in Germany. Excellent bittering quality, especially suited to darker, stronger ales and lagers. It is likely that Northdown will replace this hop.

## Aroma hops

These are varieties that have a low acid content, but possess superb aroma and flavouring qualities. Aroma hops can be used in the copper, as a bittering hop, but because the alpha acid is low they are quite expensive to use which is why many breweries have cut back or stopped using them.

**GOLDINGS** – beautiful, flowery aroma. Now being widely replaced with the less assertive aromas of CHALLENGER and MOUNT HOOD.

**FUGGLES** – traditionally used for bittering and aroma, but due to a gradual reduction in the acid content it is not practical to use them in the copper. Although the aroma is less delicate than Goldings they impart a fine flavour when added late

19

in the boil. Although English-grown Fuggles are now rather scarce, they are widely grown in the USA and are of a high quality.

**WGV (WHITBREAD GOLDING VARIETY)** – has a flavour somewhere between a Fuggle and a Golding but with a slightly higher bittering power. Best blended with other varieties in bitters and pale ales.

**BRAMLING CROSS** – a cross-bred Golding possessing some traditional Golding characteristics. Like WGV it is best blended with other varieties to get the best from it.

**PROGRESS** – a very versatile hop, with a good flavour and aroma to complement the respectable alpha acid level. This is another hop that seems to benefit from being blended with other varieties.

**WILLAMETTE** – an American hop grown from English Fuggles stock. A very fine aroma hop that can be used in any recipe calling for Fuggles. Many British breweries are now incorporating Willamette into their recipes where a good hop character is required.

**MOUNT HOOD** – although grown from Halletauer stock, Mount Hood also possesses much of the Goldings character, making it a very versatile hop. Excellent for aroma in ales and for bittering lagers.

**STYRIAN GOLDING** – actually a Fuggle grown seedless in the former Yugoslavia, but the different growing conditions have given it a different character that makes it suitable for many applications. Has an excellent aroma and is well suited to British bitters and pale ales.

**HALLETAUER** – classic German aroma hop. Although it is very low in alpha acid, it is high in the essential oils which provide flavour and aroma.

**TETTNANG** – a German hop with excellent aroma qualities.

**SAAZ** – the classic pilsner hop from the Czech Republic, which is widely regarded as the finest hop in the world – and probably the most expensive! Superb flavour and aroma qualities.

## Dual purpose hops

These offer the best of both worlds – they have a good acid level but retain a good aroma. This means that they can be used in the copper, as a late hop or added as a dry hop.

**CHALLENGER** – probably the most widely used dual purpose hop. Originally developed as a Goldings replacement, its higher acid makes it a perfect copper hop and its fine aroma make it suitable for late additions. Many bitters, along with some other styles, are brewed entirely from Challenger.

**NORTHDOWN** – grown to replace the traditional English Northern Brewer, which has now disappeared. Northdown has a pleasant aroma that is well suited to the heavier beers. It is superb for bittering all British beers, especially stouts.

**OMEGA** – a high alpha hop with Challenger characteristics. A very fine copper hop with some aroma. Omega seems to be dying out due to lack of interest by brewers.

**BREWERS GOLD** – very popular in Germany as a copper hop. Its bitterness is highly suited to pilsners as it has no trace of harshness. Very pleasant aroma.

*Hops can deteriorate if exposed to heat or light sources, so it is important that you store them in a cool, dark place.*

# Hop weights and substitutions

All the hops required for the recipes in this book are available through the home-brew trade, but if your local shop is unable to obtain them or if they are out of stock then you can substitute one variety for another. However, because the acid content varies from one variety to another *you cannot substitute on a weight for weight basis*. For example, you can't use 80g of Target instead of 80g of Goldings, or vice versa.

- 80g of Goldings with an alpha acid content of 4% will provide 28 EBUs

- 80g of Target with an alpha acid content of 8.7% will provide 60 EBUs

(EBUs – European bittering units – refer to how bitter a beer is.)

The acid content can change from year to year, either minutely or drastically, so to ensure you produce a beer with a consistent flavour and aroma you must take these changes into account! As an example, Halletauer was listed as having atypical alpha content of 7.5%, but in the 1994 harvest the alpha acid went as low as 1.5%.Therefore if you were using a recipe including 50g of Halletauer with an alpha acid of 7.5%, then you would now need to use 250g of the 1.5% acid Halletauer to give the same level of bitterness to your brew.

To prove this:

- 50g of Halletauer with an alpha acid content of 7.5% will give 33 EBUs

- 50g of Halletauer with an alpha acid content of 1.5% will give 7 EBUs

As you can see the alpha acid content is a *very important factor* when brewing. Unfortunately the majority of wholesalers wouldn't agree and this is proved by their reluctance to print this information on their pack labels!

If you can't get a particular hop and have to select a substitute variety, then the method below shows you how to work out the new weight requirement, in grams. This method can also be used to work out the new weight of any hop if the alpha acid changes.

$$\frac{\text{weight of original hop x alpha acid of original hop}}{\text{substitute hops alpha acid or new acid content}} = \text{new weight}$$

# Yeasts

"**Most of the character of the beer is formed during the fermentation and is dependent upon the yeast.**"

*Mr Ward* (Head brewer – Fergusons)

So as you can see, the yeast strain used can be the most influential ingredient you put into your beer. Unfortunately this is the one ingredient that very few of us pay any attention to.

It is far beyond the scope of this book to go into any detail on yeasts (*see Home Brewing: The Camra Guide* by G. Wheeler which contains an excellent chapter on yeasts from reproduction to propagation).

## Dried yeast sachets

Pitifully few of these packets come with any information printed on them, again the manufacturers seem to think this information is beyond our comprehension. Always try to select a genuine top fermenting yeast – these are usually labelled as English Ale (Gervin brand) or Real Ale or just plain Ale.

The words 'genuine brewers' yeast' might look impressive on the packet, but what beer style is it for? Is it for the genuine lager brewer or the genuine ale brewer? Is it worth risking your ale for the sake of fancy, but unhelpful labelling?

## Yeast starter bottles

Activating the yeast before pitching into the brew, gives it a chance to multiply vastly, and ensures that there are adequate yeast cells to provide a rapid start to the fermentation.

A basic yeast starter method I use is:

- Dissolve 50g of dried malt extract (easier to work with when using small quantities) in half a pint of boiling water. Then, taking extreme care not to tip it over yourself, pour the malt solution into a sterilised 1 pint beer bottle and plug the neck with unmedicated cotton wool.

- When the solution has cooled to room temperature, remove the cotton wool, cover with your hand, and shake well. Then add your packet (preferably 2 packets) of yeast, and replug the neck with the cotton wool.

- Only add the starter to your beer when a good frothy head has appeared, remembering to check your wort is at the correct temperature as well.

## Bottle conditioned beers

Many breweries now produce beers that are bottle conditioned, this gives the home brewer the chance to use a brewery's yeast. When looking for a bottle conditioned beer to use, try to select the one with a good ring of sediment in the bottle.

To use the yeast from such a bottle, make up the starter solution as above, then carefully pour the contents of the bottle into a glass (the idea is to leave the sediment behind), leaving about 100ml in the bottle. Cover the brewery bottle with your hand and give it a good shake, then pour the cloudy remains into your starter solution and continue as for a packet yeast.

## Liquid yeast cultures

These are becoming available to the home brewer in wider selections. Wyeast (via Brupaks) foil packs contain a pure strain of yeast in an inner membrane and an outer membrane of a starter medium. To use, simply strike the bag to burst the inner membrane, wait for the pack to expand and then pitch.

The method Brupaks recommend for reculturing Wyeast should be carried out with utmost care as it would be all too easy to spoil the yeast. Perhaps it might be better to bottle a couple of pints and hold these in reserve, then treat them as you would a brewery bottle conditioned beer.

# Malt extract instructions: method no. 1

*No mash required – use any unhopped light coloured extract*

With this method, only the recipes that use pale malt, crystal malt, black malt, chocolate malt, Carapils malt and brewing sugars may be brewed. No mash is required, so the pale malt can be replaced with a light-coloured non-diastatic malt extract and the ingredients are simply boiled together in your boiler.

1. Pour 18 litres of water into your boiler and bring it to 40–50°C.

2. Briefly turn off the heat and add the malt extract and the grains stirring well, turn the heat back on and bring to the boil.

3. When the wort comes to the boil add the first batch of hops.

4. Halfway through the boil add any sugars which the recipe calls for.

5. In the last 15 minutes add the Irish moss and the late hops.

6. If you have a strainer fitted, let the wort stand for 30 minutes and then run the wort into the fermenter. Those not using a strainer will have to carefully tip the wort into a hop back and let the hops act as a filter there.

7. Let the wort cool to 25–30°C. Preferably this should be done as quickly as possible to eliminate any risk of infection. You can stand the bin in a larger vessel containing cold water, stirring regularly, to allow the temperature to even out. Alternatively, Brupaks manufacture immersible wort chillers which cool the wort to pitching temperature in about 20 minutes. This precipitates protein as 'trub' and the clear wort should be racked off the sediment.

8. Top up to 23 litres, if necessary, with cold water and when cool stir the wort well, or tip it from one vessel to another to aerate it. Yeast needs oxygen present to allow it to start the fermentation and multiply.

9. Pitch the yeast. Once the yeast head has formed, skim off any hop debris. After this there should be no need for further skimming.

10. After 48 hours carefully syphon the wort into another vessel, leaving behind as much sediment as possible. A new yeast head will quickly form. This step is optional, but it does improve quality.

11. When the final gravity is met, siphon the beer into your pressure barrel and add 50g of priming sugar, preferably malt extract.

**Bottling** is best effected once the beer has fallen clear and had some maturing time in the cask. Those who wish the beer to come into condition quickly once bottled should add half a teaspoon of sugar per 500ml bottle.

12. Mature the beer for as long as possible, allow 1 week for every 10 degrees as a minimum e.g. 1040 = 4 weeks, 1060 = 6 weeks.

# Malt extract instructions: method no. 2

*Partial mash – diastatic malt extract required*

All recipes can be brewed, the pale malt is replaced with a diastatic malt extract and no mash tun is required.

1. Pour 18 litres of water into your boiler and heat to 40–50°C.

2. Briefly turn off the heat and add the malt extract and the grains, stirring well. Turn the heat back on.

3. Slowly raise the temperature to 66°C and maintain this temperature for 30 minutes. Ensure the temperature does not exceed 70°C – cold water can be added as an emergency cooler.

4. Slowly raise the temperature to 75°C and then bring to the boil as fast as you can.

5. When the wort comes to the boil add the first batch of hops.

6. Halfway through the boil add any sugars which the recipe calls for.

7. In the last 15 minutes add the Irish moss and the late hops.

8. If you have a strainer fitted let the wort stand for 30 minutes and then run the wort into the fermenter, otherwise carefully tip the wort into a hop back and let the hops act as a filter there.

9. Let the wort cool to 25–30°C. Preferably this should be done as quickly as possible to eliminate any risk of infection. You can stand the bin in a larger

vessel containing cold water, stirring regularly, to allow the temperature to even out. Alternatively Brupaks manufacture immersible wort chillers which cool the wort to pitching temperature in about 20 minutes. This precipitates protein as 'trub' and the clear wort should be racked off.

10. Top up to 23 litres, if necessary, with cold water and when cool stir the wort well or tip it from one vessel to another to aerate it. Yeast needs oxygen present to allow it to start the fermentation and multiply.

11. Pitch the yeast. Once the yeast head has formed, skim off any hop debris and trub. After this there should be no need for further skimming.

12. After 48 hours carefully siphon the wort into another vessel, leaving behind as much sediment as possible. A new yeast head will quickly form. This step is optional, but it does improve quality.

13. When the final gravity is met, siphon the beer into your pressure barrel and add 50g of priming sugar, preferably malt extract.

**Bottling** is best effected once the beer has fallen clear and had some maturing time in the cask. Those who wish the beer to come into condition quickly once bottled should add half a teaspoon of sugar per 500ml bottle.

14. Mature the beer for as long as possible, allow 1 week for every 10 degrees as a minimum e.g. 1040 = 4 weeks, 1060 = 6 weeks.

# All grain instructions

*Full mash required*

All the recipes in this book were formulated around this method. Mashing will take you closer to emulating the commercial than the other methods.

1. Bring the mash liquor to a strike heat of 72°C.

2. Add the grains and adjuncts, stirring constantly to avoid any dry pockets of grain forming.

3. Check the mash is at the correct temperature, if it isn't quickly adjust it by adding boiling water, again stirring all the time.

4. Fit the tun lid and leave to mash for the required amount of time. Occasionally check the temperature, if it falls too low add more boiling water and remember to check the insulating properties of your tun before brewing again. While the mash is occurring, check you have adequate supply of sparge water and keep its temperature between 77–80°C.

5. Once the mash is complete, open the tap on your tun and let the wort run very slowly into the boiler. The first few litres of running may be cloudy and they should be returned to the tun, carefully. When the element is covered turn your boiler on.

6. Once the run-off has nearly finished, slowly sparge to rinse out any trapped sugars in the spent grains. Continue to sparge until the gravity is below 5 degrees.

7. Bring the wort to the boil.

8. When the wort comes to the boil add the first batch of hops.

9. Halfway through the boil add any sugars which the recipe calls for.

10. In the last 15 minutes add the Irish moss and the late hops.

11. If you have a strainer fitted let the wort stand for 30 minutes and then run the wort into the fermenter, otherwise carefully tip the wort into a hop back and let the hops act as a filter there.

12. Let the wort cool to 25–30°C. Preferably this should be done as quickly as possible to eliminate any risk of infection. You can stand the bin in a larger vessel containing cold water, stirring regularly, to allow the temperature to even out. Alternatively Brupaks manufacture immersible wort chillers which cool the wort to pitching temperature in about 20 minutes. This precipitates protein as 'trub' and the clear wort should be racked off the sediment.

13. Top up to 23 litres, if necessary, with cold water and when cool stir the wort well or tip it from one vessel to another to aerate it. Yeast needs oxygen to allow it to start the fermentation and multiply.

14. Pitch the yeast. Once the yeast head has formed, skim off any hop debris and trub. After this there should be no need for further skimming.

15. After 48 hours carefully siphon the wort into another vessel, leaving behind as much sediment as possible. A new yeast head will quickly form. This step is optional, but it does improve quality.

16. When the final gravity is met siphon the beer into your pressure barrel and add 50g of priming sugar, preferably malt extract.

**Bottling** is best effected once the beer has fallen clear and had some maturing time in the cask. Those who wish the beer to come into condition quickly once bottled should add half a teaspoon of sugar per 500ml bottle.

17. Mature the beer for as long as possible, allow 1 week for every 10 degrees as a minimum e.g. 1040 =4 weeks, 1060 =6 weeks.

# Recipe formulations

No imperial equivalents to weights and measures were used as it seems that kilograms and litres are now becoming universally accepted, and because more and more products are appearing in a metric-only form.

While many of the recipes were brewed and tasted with the aid of an overworked mash tun/boiler, and the help of customers and friends, all recipes were formulated with a computer to meet the brewers' original gravities and bitterness levels expressed in European Bittering Units (EBUs).

To allow even the most inexperienced brewer to achieve good results, the mash efficiency for the recipes was set at 75%. In some cases you might find you constantly exceed the final volume of 23 litres, if this is the case you can reduce the ingredients slightly.

**MASH LIQUOR** quantities were based on 2.5 litres per kg of grist.

**MASH TEMPERATURE** was estimated. Providing you keep the temperature between 62°C and 68°C you will get a good beer.

**BOIL PERIOD** – hop weights were based on a minimum boil of 90 minutes being used. A 2-hour boil isn't necessary but it does improve the keeping qualities of the final beer.

**FINAL GRAVITY** and **ABV %** are affected by the mash temperature, among other things, so these figures are for guidance only, although in test brews they did prove accurate.

**FINAL VOLUME** – this is how many litres of beer should end up in your barrel.

**HOPS** – to match the brewer's level of bitterness, measured in EBUs, the hop weights were calculated using a 20% extraction efficiency and a minimum boil of

90 minutes. Where the EBU was unavailable it was estimated. The figure in brackets, after the hop variety, was the alpha acid level of the hops used to formulate the hop weights for that recipe.

Some breweries use hop extracts and pellets. Where this is the case the extract has been substituted with Target hops, and whole hops replace the pellets.

**LATE HOPS** – weights were based on between 15-20% of the combined weights of the copper hops.

**DRY HOPS** – weights were estimated.

# The recipes

## Belhaven Brewery Co.

### BELHAVEN 70/-

*Excellent and delectable honey-coloured session beer with a pleasing hop aroma*

| | | | |
|---|---|---|---|
| Original gravity: | 1035 | Mash liquor: | 10 litres |
| Final gravity: | 1008 | Mash temperature: | 65ºC |
| Alcohol content: | 3.50% | Mash time: | 90 minutes |
| Bittering units: | 23 | Boil time: | 90 minutes |
| Final volume: | 23 litres | | |

In the tun

| | |
|---|---|
| Pale malt | 3610g |
| Crystal malt | 80g |
| Black malt | 40g |

In the boiler

| | |
|---|---|
| WGV hops (4.5%) | 64g (start of boil) |
| Invert sugar | 196g (after 45 minutes) |
| Fuggles hops | 5g (last 15 minutes) |
| Goldings hops | 8g (last 15 minutes) |
| Irish Moss | 5g (last 15 minutes) |

Malt extract version
No mash required Replace the pale malt with 2650g of light-coloured malt extract.

# Belhaven Brewery Co.

## BELHAVEN 60/-

*A fine example of a dark mild, full malt flavour in the mouth with light hop notes.*

| | | | |
|---|---|---|---|
| Original gravity: | 1031 | Mash liquor: | 8 litres |
| Final gravity: | 1007 | Mash temperature: | 63ºC |
| Alcohol content: | 3.00% | Mash time: | 90 minutes |
| Bittering units: | 21 | Boil time: | 90 minutes |
| Final volume: | 23 litres | | |

### In the tun
| | |
|---|---|
| Pale malt | 2980g |
| Crystal malt | 65g |
| Black malt | 65g |

### In the boiler
| | |
|---|---|
| WGV hops (4.5%) | 58g (start of boil) |
| Invert sugar | 234g (after 45 minutes) |
| Fuggles hops | 5g (last 15 minutes) |
| Goldings hops | 7g (last 15 minutes) |
| Irish Moss | 5g (last 15 minutes) |

### Notes
Belhaven blend old traditional brewing methods with newer technology, enabling them to produce distinctive ales. Some of their beers are available bottled via supermarkets such as Asda and Safeway.

### Malt extract version
No mash required. Replace the pale malt with 2200g of light-coloured malt extract.

## Belhaven Brewery Co.

# SANDY HUNTER'S TRADITIONAL ALE

*A unique blend of malt, hops and heritage which celebrates Sandy Hunter, erstwhile chairman and brewer of Belhaven for over 35 years. Full malt and nutty palate with distinctive nose and flavour*

| | | | |
|---|---|---|---|
| Original gravity: | 1038 | Mash liquor: | 10 litres |
| Final gravity: | 1010 | Mash temperature: | 65ºC |
| Alcohol content: | 3.60% | Mash time: | 90 minutes |
| Bittering units: | 25 | Boil time: | 90 minutes |
| Final volume: | 23 litres | | |

**36**

### In the tun
| | |
|---|---|
| Pale malt | 3860g |
| Crystal malt | 85g |
| Black malt | 40g |

### In the boiler
| | |
|---|---|
| WGV hops (4.5%) | 69g (start of boil) |
| Invert sugar | 210g (after 45 minutes) |
| Fuggles hops | 7g (last 15 minutes) |
| Goldings hops | 7g (last 15 minutes) |
| Irish Moss | 5g (last 15 minutes) |

Malt extract version
No mash required. Replace the pale malt with 2800g of light-coloured malt extract

# Belhaven Brewery Co.

## BELHAVEN 80/-

*A good example of an 80/- ale. A memorably rounded ale, with a complex mix of grain and hop, producing Belhaven's easily recognized flavour*

| | | | |
|---|---|---|---|
| Original gravity: | 1042 | Mash liquor: | 11 litres |
| Final gravity: | 1010 | Mash temperature: | 65°C |
| Alcohol content : | 4.10% | Mash time: | 90 minutes |
| Bittering unit: | 29 | Boil time: | 90 minutes |
| Final volume: | 23 litres | | |

In the tun

| | |
|---|---|
| Pale malt | 3865g |
| Crystal malt | 110g |
| Black malt | 70g |

In the boiler

| | |
|---|---|
| WGV hops (4.5%) | 81g (start of boil) |
| Invert sugar | 449g (after 45 minutes) |
| Fuggles hops | 6g (last 15 minutes) |
| Goldings hops | 10g (last 15 minutes) |
| Irish Moss | 5g (last 15 minutes) |

Malt extract version

No mash required. Replace the pale malt with 2800g of light-coloured malt extract.

## Belhaven Brewery Co.

# St ANDREWS ALE

*The use of dry hops adds much to the character of this ale.*

| | | |
|---|---|---|
| Original gravity: | 1046 | Mash liquor: 12 litres |
| Final gravity: | 1011 | Mash temperature: 66°C |
| Alcohol content: | 4.50% | Mash time: 90 minutes |
| Bittering units: | 36 | Boil time: 2 hours |
| Final volume: | 23 litres | |

### In the tun

| | |
|---|---|
| Pale malt | 4285g |
| Crystal malt | 125g |
| Black malt | 75g |

### In the boiler

| | |
|---|---|
| WGV hops (4.5%) | 100g (start of boil) |
| Invert sugar | 498g (after 1 hour) |
| Fuggles hops | 8g (last 15 minutes) |
| Goldings hops | 12g (last 15 minutes) |
| Irish Moss | 5g (last 15 minutes) |

### Malt extract version

No mash required. Replace the pale malt with 3150g of light-coloured malt extract.

## Belhaven Brewery Co.

# BELHAVEN 90/-

*Potent old ale, you should preferably bottle this in nip size bottles.*

| | | | |
|---|---|---|---|
| Original gravity: | 1070 | Mash liquor: 18 litres | |
| Final gravity: | 1012 | Mash temperature: 66ºC | |
| Alcohol content: | 7.50% | Mash time: 2 hours | |
| Bittering units: | 34 | Boil time: 2 hours | |
| Final volume: | 23 litres | | |

### In the tun

| | |
|---|---|
| Pale malt | 6320g |
| Black malt | 300 g |

### In the boiler

| | |
|---|---|
| WGV hops (4.5%) | 94g (start of boil) |
| Invert sugar | 902g (after 1 hour) |
| Fuggles hops | 5g (last 15 minutes) |
| Goldings hops | 12 g (last 15 minutes) |
| Irish Moss | 5g (last 15 minutes) |

Malt extract version

No mash required. Replace the pale malt with 4600g of light-coloured malt extract.

## Borve Brew House

# BORVE ALE

*The use of Omega hops and roast barley add much to the aroma and tastw. This ale is well worth a brew as it is packed with malt and hop character.*

| | | | |
|---|---|---|---|
| Original gravity: | 1040 | Mash liquor: | 11 litres |
| Final gravity: | 1011 | Mash temperature: | 65°C |
| Alcohol content: | 3.70% | Mash time: | 90 minutes |
| Bittering units: | 26 | Boil time: | 90 minutes |
| Final volume: | 23 litres | | |

In the tun

| | |
|---|---|
| Pale malt | 4380g |
| Chocolate malt | 25g |
| Crystal malt | 70g |
| Roast Barley | 45g |

In the boiler

| | |
|---|---|
| Target hop (8.7%) | 22 g (start of boil) |
| Omega hops (8.5%) | 15 g (start of boil) |
| Omega hops | 8 g (last 15 minutes) |
| Irish Moss | 5 g (last 15 minutes) |

Notes:
Substitute Omega with 21g of Challenger (6.2%) if unavailable. Borve use hop pellets.

Malt extract version
No mash required. Replace the pale malt with 3200g of light-coloured malt extract.

Borve Brew House

# TALL SHIPS INDIA PALE ALE

| | | | |
|---|---|---|---|
| Original gravity: | 1050 | Mash liquor: | 14 litres |
| Final gravity: | 1012 | Mash temperature: | 66ºC |
| Alcohol content: | 4.90% | Mash time: | 90 minutes |
| Bittering units: | 20 | Boil time: | 2 hours |
| Final volume: | 23 litres | | |

### In the tun
| | |
|---|---|
| Pale malt | 5580g |
| Crystal malt | 40g |
| Chocolate malt | 15g |

### In the boiler
| | |
|---|---|
| Omega hops (8.5%) | 29g (start of boil) |
| Halletauer hops | 6g (last 15 minutes) |
| Irish Moss | 5g (last 15 minutes) |

### Notes:
Substitute Omega hops with 40g of Challenger (6.2%), if unavailable. The brewary uses hop pellets.

### Malt extract version
No mash required. Replace the pale malt with 4100g of light-coloured malt extract.

## Borve Brew House

# ABERDEEN UNION STREET 200

| | | | |
|---|---|---|---|
| Original gravity: | 1050 | Mash liquor: | 14 litres |
| Final gravity: | 1011 | Mash temperature: | 66°C |
| Alcohol content: | 5.00% | Mash time: | 90 minutes |
| Bittering units: | 20 | Boil time: | 2 hours |
| Final volume: | 23 litres | | |

In the tun

| | |
|---|---|
| Pale malt | 5315g |
| Crystal malt | 115g |
| Roast barley | 225g |

In the boiler

| | |
|---|---|
| Target hops (8.7%) | 29g (start of boil) |
| Halletauer hops | 6g (last 15 minutes) |
| Irish Moss | 5g (last 15 minutes) |

Malt extract version

No mash required. Replace the pale malt with 3900g of light-coloured malt extract.

## Harviestoun Brewery

# WAVERLEY 70/-

*A chestnut-coloured session brew with great drinkability. It is crisp and hoppy with a good balance of roast malt flavour and Progress and Goldings hops. Voted Best Beer at several festivals.*

| | | | |
|---|---|---|---|
| Original gravity: | 1037 | Mash liquor: | 10 litres |
| Final gravity: | 1008 | Mash temperature: | 65ºC |
| Alcohol content: | 3.70% | Mash time: | 90 minutes |
| Bittering units: | 25 | Boil time: | 90 minutes |
| Final volume: | 23 litres | | |

### In the tun
| | |
|---|---|
| Pale malt | 3435g |
| Crystal malt | 325g |
| Roast barley | 40g |

### In the boiler
| | |
|---|---|
| Progress hops (5.5%) | 57g (start of boil) |
| Soft brown sugar | 242g (after 45 minutes) |
| Goldings hops | 11g (last 15 minutes) |
| Irish Moss | 5g (last 15 minutes) |
| Goldings hops | 5g (dry hops in cask) |

### Notes
Harviestoun add hop oil, instead of whole hops, to the cask. Ken Brooker, the brewery owner and brewer, was once an avid home brewer whose ales were so well liked he set up a brewery and had to expand in the early 1990s! Proof – if any were needed – that home brewers can produce ales to be proud of.

### Malt extract version
No mash required. Replace the pale malt with 2500g of light-coloured malt extract.

## Harviestoun Brewery

# ORIGINAL 80/-

*A good example of a best Scotch Ale but with more emphasis on the hops than other beers produced in Scotland. This beer was chosen by Michael Jackson as one of his 'best beers of Britain'.*

| | | | |
|---|---|---|---|
| Original gravity: | 1041 | Mash liquor: | 11 litres |
| Final gravity: | 1009 | Mash temperature: | 65ºC |
| Alcohol content: | 4.10% | Mash time: | 90 minutes |
| Bittering units: | 24 | Boil time: | 90 minutes |
| Final volume: | 23 litres | | |

In the tun
| | |
|---|---|
| Pale malt | 3805g |
| Crystal malt | 405g |

In the boiler
| | |
|---|---|
| Fuggles hops (3.3%) | 91g (start of boil) |
| Soft brown sugar | 234g (after 45 minutes) |
| Goldings hops | 18 g (last 15 minutes) |
| Irish Moss | 5g (last 15 minutes) |
| Goldings hops | 7 g (dry hops in cask) |

Notes:
Harviestoun add hop oil, instead of whole hops, to the cask.

Malt extract version
No mash required. Replace the pale malt with 2800g of light-coloured malt extract.

## Harviestoun Brewery

# MONTROSE ALE

*A rich fruity beer which is well balanced and packed with flavour.*

| | | | |
|---|---|---|---|
| Original gravity: | 1042 | Mash liquor: | 12 litres |
| Final gravity: | 1009 | Mash temperature: | 65°C |
| Alcohol content: | 4.20% | Mash time: | 90 minutes |
| Bittering units: | 22 | Boil time: | 90 minutes |
| Final volume: | 23 litres | | |

In the tun
| | |
|---|---|
| Pale malt | 4235g |
| Crystal malt | 380g |
| Chocolate malt | 95g |

In the boiler
| | |
|---|---|
| Fuggles hops (3.3%) | 83g (start of boil) |
| Molasses | 48g (after 45 minutes) |
| Goldings hops | 17g (last 15 minutes) |
| Irish Moss | 5g (last 15 minutes) |
| Goldings hops | 2g (dry hops in cask) |

Notes:
Harviestoun add hop oil, instead of whole hops, to the cask

Malt extract version
No mash required. Replace the pale malt with 3100g of light-coloured malt extract.

## Harviestoun Brewery

# PTARMIGAN

*Introduced in 1992 and very popular. A golden ale with an appealing bouquet from the Saaz hops.*

| | | | |
|---|---|---|---|
| Original gravity: | 1045 | Mash liquor: | 12 litres |
| Final gravity: | 1010 | Mash temperature: | 65°C |
| Alcohol content: | 4.50% | Mash time: | 90 minutes |
| Bittering units: | 26 | Boil time: | 90 minutes |
| Final volume: | 23 litres | | |

In the tun

| | |
|---|---|
| Pale malt | 4440g |
| Crystal malt | 200g |
| Wheat malt | 200g |

In the boiler

| | |
|---|---|
| Saaz hops (1.5%) | 217g (start of boil) |
| White sugar | 150g (after 45 minutes) |
| Saaz hops | 43g (last 15 minutes) |
| Irish Moss | 5g (last 15 minutes) |
| Saaz hops | 10 g (dry hops in cask) |

Notes:
Harviestoun add hop oil, instead of whole hops, to the cask. Saaz had a particularly low acid when the recipe was formulated, so check what acid is currently available and, if necessary, recalculate hop weight.

Malt extract version
Partial mash required. Replace the pale malt with 3250g of diastatic malt extract.

## Harviestoun Brewery

# SCHIEHALLION

*Brewed using the finest lager malt and hops, fermented at low temperatures and served 'on the yeast' at cellar temperatures without the extra fizz! A well-balanced full-flavoured beer.*

| | | | |
|---|---|---|---|
| Original gravity: | 1048 | Mash liquor | : 14 litres |
| Final gravity: | 1011 | Mash temperature | : 65ºC |
| Alcohol content: | 4.80% | Mash time | : 90 minutes |
| Bittering units: | 28 | Boil time | : 90 minutes |
| Final volume: | 23 litres | | |

In the tun

| | |
|---|---|
| Lager malt | 5145g |
| Wheat malt | 270g |

In the boiler

| | |
|---|---|
| Challenger hops (6.2%) | 34g (start of boil) |
| Halletauer hops (1.5%) | 93 g (start of boil) |
| Halletauer hops | 25g (last 15 minutes) |
| Irish Moss | 5g (last 15 minutes) |

Notes:
This beer is unique in as much as it is the only cask-conditioned lager in this book and probably the only one in the UK. I recommend a bottom fermenting yeast is used for this beer and that you use lower fermenting temperatures (5°C–14°C).

Malt extract version
Partial mash required. Replace the pale malt with 3750g of diastatic malt extract.

## Harviestoun Brewery

# OLD MANOR

*A well balanced ale, full of character and a great Goldings aroma.*

| | | | |
|---|---|---|---|
| Original gravity: | 1050 | Mash liquor: | 14 litres |
| Final gravity: | 1011 | Mash temperature: | 66°C |
| Alcohol content: | 5.00% | Mash time: | 90 minutes |
| Bittering units: | 24 | Boil time: | 2 hours |
| Final volume: | 23 litres | | |

In the tun

| | |
|---|---|
| Pale malt | 4920g |
| Crystal malt | 220g |
| Chocolate malt | 55g |

In the boiler

| | |
|---|---|
| Northern Brewer hops (5.7%) | 37g (start of boil) |
| Goldings hops (4.0%) | 23g (start of boil) |
| Soft brown sugar | 273 g (after 1 hour) |
| Goldings hops | 12g (last 15 minutes) |
| Irish Moss | 5g (last 15 minutes) |
| Goldings hops | 10g (dry hops in cask) |

Notes:
Harviestoun use hop oil instead of whole hops in the cask.

Malt extract version
No mash required. Replace the pale malt with 3600g of light-coloured malt extract.

Maclay & Co.

# MACLAY 70/-

*Pleasant copper coloured ale with a light hop aroma and a tasty balance of malt and hops.*

| | | | |
|---|---|---|---|
| Original gravity: | 1036 | Mash liquor | : 10 litres |
| Final gravity: | 1008 | Mash temperature | : 65ºC |
| Alcohol content: | 3.60% | Mash time | : 90 minutes |
| Bittering units: | 33 | Boil time | : 90 minutes |
| Final volume: | 23 litres | | |

In the tun

| | |
|---|---|
| Pale malt | 3680g |
| Crystal malt | 205g |
| Wheat malt | 205g |

In the boiler

| | |
|---|---|
| Fuggles hops (3.3%) | 125g (start of boil) |
| Brewers Gold hops | 25g (last 15 minutes) |
| Irish Moss | 5g (last 15 minutes) |

Malt extract version
Partial mash required. Replace the pale malt with 2700g of diastatic malt extract.

## Maclay & Co.

# BROADSWORD

*A very refreshing beer, the Fuggles give a good hop character whilst the Styrian Goldings give a superb aroma. The use of carapils ensures this beer has a good body, slight residual sweetness and a very pale colour.*

| | | | |
|---|---|---|---|
| Original gravity: | 1038 | Mash liquor: | 11 litres |
| Final gravity: | 1009 | Mash temperature: | 65ºC |
| Alcohol content: | 3.80% | Mash time: | 90 minutes |
| Bittering units: | 36 | Boil time: | 90 minutes |
| Final volume: | 23 litres | | |

### In the tun
| | |
|---|---|
| Pale malt | 3830g |
| Carapils malt | 475g |

### In the boiler
| | |
|---|---|
| Fuggles hops (3.3%) | 136g (start of boil) |
| Styrian Golding hops | 27g (last 15 minutes) |
| Irish Moss | 5g (last 15 minutes) |

### Notes
For Broadsword, Maclay use malted oats which can add a creaminess to the ale. Due to the scarcity of this ingredient in the home-brew market it has been omitted from this recipe, however, it is still an excellent ale. If you can obtain and wish to use this ingredient, then reduce the pale malt by 645g and replace with malted oats.

### Malt extract version
No mash required. Replace the pale malt with 2800g of light-coloured malt extract.

## Maclay & Co.

# KANE'S AMBER ALE

*A pleasing balance of malt and hops makes this beer a treat to drink.*

| | | | |
|---|---|---|---|
| Original gravity: | 1040 | Mash liquor: | 11 litres |
| Final gravity: | 1009 | Mash temperature: | 65ºC |
| Alcohol content: | 4.00% | Mash time: | 90 minutes |
| Bittering units: | 30 | Boil time: | 2 hours |
| Final volume: | 23 litres | | |

In the tun

| | | |
|---|---|---|
| Pale malt | 4085 | g |
| Wheat malt | 230 | g |
| Crystal malt | 230 | g |

In the boiler

| | |
|---|---|
| Fuggles hops (3.3%) | 114g (start of boil) |
| Fuggles hops | 24g (last 15 minutes) |
| Irish Moss | 5g (last 15 minutes) |

Malt extract version
Partial mash required. Replace the pale malt with 3000g of diastatic malt extract.

## Maclay & Co.

# MACLAY SCOTCH ALE

*A mid gold-coloured ale with a slightly sweet malty edge, nicely balanced by the hops.*

| | | | |
|---|---|---|---|
| Original gravity: | 1050 | Mash liquor: | 14 litres |
| Final gravity: | 1011 | Mash temperature: | 65°C |
| Alcohol content: | 5.00% | Mash time: | 90 minutes |
| Bittering units: | 35 | Boil time: | 90 minutes |
| Final volume: | 23 litres | | |

In the tun
| | |
|---|---|
| Pale malt | 5090g |
| Wheat malt | 285g |
| Carapils malt | 285g |

In the boiler
| | |
|---|---|
| Fuggles hops (3.3%) | 133g (start of boil) |
| Fuggles hops | 27g (last 15 minutes) |
| Irish Moss | 5g (last 15 minutes) |

Malt extract version
Partial mash required. Replace the pale malt with 3700g of diastatic malt extract.

## Orkney Brewery

# RAVEN ALE

*Stunning balance of malt, hop and fruit with a complex finish of hoppy dryness and roast barley nuttiness.*

| | | | |
|---|---|---|---|
| Original gravity: | 1038 | Mash liquor: | 11 litres |
| Final gravity: | 1009 | Mash temperature: | 65°C |
| Alcohol content: | 3.80% | Mash time: | 90 minutes |
| Bittering units: | 18 | Boil time: | 90 minutes |
| Final volume: | 23 litres | | |

In the tun

| | |
|---|---|
| Pale malt | 3965g |
| Chocolate malt | 45g |
| Crystal malt | 130g |
| Torrified wheat | 170g |

In the boiler

| | |
|---|---|
| WGV hops (4.5%) | 50g (start of boil) |
| Goldings hops | 10g (last 15 minutes) |
| Irish Moss | 5g (last 15 minutes) |

Notes:
This is Britain's most northerly brewery.

Malt extract version
Partial mash required. Replace the pale malt with 2900g of diastatic malt extract.

## Orkney Brewery

# DRAGONHEAD STOUT

*A good honest, no-nonsense stout with a smooth, clean refreshing taste, bursting with the flavours of the different coloured malts.*

| | | | |
|---|---|---|---|
| Original gravity: | 1040 | Mash liquor: | 12 litres |
| Final gravity: | 1008 | Mash temperature: | 66ºC |
| Alcohol content: | 4.10% | Mash time: | 2 hours |
| Bittering units: | 29 | Boil time: | 2 hours |
| Final volume: | 23 litres | | |

In the tun

| | |
|---|---|
| Pale malt | 4080g |
| Crystal malt | 90g |
| Roast Barley | 135g |
| Black malt | 45g |
| Torrified wheat | 135g |

In the boiler

| | |
|---|---|
| Omega hops (8.5%) | 44g (start of boil) |
| White cane sugar | 45 g (after 1 hour) |
| Goldings hops | 10g (last 15 minutes) |
| Irish Moss | 5g (last 15 minutes) |

Notes:
Substitute Omega with 60g of Challenger (6.2%) if unavailable

Malt extract version
Partial mash required. Replace the pale malt with 3000g of diastatic malt extract.

## Orkney Brewery

# DARK ISLAND

*A rich wine-coloured ale, which is rounded and refreshing in the mouth, with a good malt and hop balance.*

| | | | |
|---|---|---|---|
| Original gravity: | 1045 | Mash liquor: | 12 litres |
| Final gravity: | 1009 | Mash temperature: | 65°C |
| Alcohol content: | 4.70% | Mash time: | 90 minutes |
| Bittering units: | 22 | Boil time: | 90 minutes |
| Final volume: | 23 litres | | |

In the tun

| | |
|---|---|
| Pale malt | 4170g |
| Chocolate malt | 150g |
| Crystal malt | 150g |
| Torrified wheat | 50g |

In the boiler

| | |
|---|---|
| Omega hops (8.5%) | 32g (start of boil) |
| White cane sugar | 294g (after 45 minutes) |
| Challenger hops | 6g (last 15 minutes) |
| Irish Moss | 5g (last 15 minutes) |

Notes:
Substitute Omega with 44g of Challenger (6.2%) if unavailable.

Malt extract version
Partial mash required. Replace the pale malt with 3050g of diastatic malt extract.

## Orkney Brewery

# SKULLSPLITTER

*A reddish ale with a smooth and dangerous drinkability! It has a great satiny 'malt in the mouth' feel.*

| | | | |
|---|---|---|---|
| Original gravity: | 1080 | Mash liquor: | 18 litres |
| Final gravity: | 1014 | Mash temperature: | 67°C |
| Alcohol content: | 8.50% | Mash time: | 2 hours |
| Bittering units: | 20 | Boil time: | 2 hours |
| Final volume: | 23 litres | | |

In the tun

| | |
|---|---|
| Pale malt | 7710g |
| Chocolate malt | 90g |
| Crystal malt | 265g |
| Torrified wheat | 265g |

In the boiler

| | |
|---|---|
| WGV hops (4.5%) | 56g (start of boil) |
| White cane sugar | 438g (after 1 hour) |
| Goldings hops | 11g (last 15 minutes) |
| Irish Moss | 5g (last 15 minutes) |

Malt extract version
Partial mash required. Replace the pale malt with 5650g of diastatic malt extract.

Tomintoul Brewery

# TOMINTOUL CAILLIE

*By Scottish standards this beer has a high level of bitterness which fills your mouth. A great thirst quencher, loaded with character.*

| | | | |
|---|---|---|---|
| Original gravity: | 1036 | Mash liquor: | 10 litres |
| Final gravity: | 1008 | Mash temperature: | 65ºC |
| Alcohol content: | 3.60% | Mash time: | 90 minutes |
| Bittering units: | 40 | Boil time: | 2 hours |
| Final volume: | 23 litres | | |

In the tun

| | |
|---|---|
| Pale malt | 3835g |
| Crystal malt | 245g |

In the boiler

| | |
|---|---|
| Challenger hops (6.2%) | 81g (start of boil) |
| Goldings hops | 6 g (last 15 minutes) |
| Irish Moss | 5g (last 15 minutes) |

Malt extract version
No mash required. Replace the pale malt with 2800g of light-coloured malt extract.

## Tomintoul Brewery

# TOMINTOUL WILD CAT

*Test brews proved this to be a full bodied ale with the Fuggles giving a tangy hop flavour. Well worth a brew.*

| | | | |
|---|---|---|---|
| Original gravity: | 1050 | Mash liquor: | 14 litres |
| Final gravity: | 1010 | Mash temperature: | 66°C |
| Alcohol content: | 5.10% | Mash time: | 90 minutes |
| Bittering units: | 25 | Boil time: | 90 minutes |
| Final volume: | 23 litres | | |

In the tun

| | |
|---|---|
| Pale malt | 5315g |
| Crystal malt | 225g |
| Chocolate malt | 55g |

In the boiler

| | |
|---|---|
| Northdown hops (7.5%) | 42g (start of boil) |
| Fuggles hops | 8g (last 15 minutes) |
| Irish Moss | 5g (last 15 minutes) |

Malt extract version
No mash required. Replace the pale malt with 3900g of light-coloured malt extract.

Tomintoul Brewery

## TOMINTOUL STAG

| | | | |
|---|---|---|---|
| Original gravity: | 1040 | Mash liquor: | 11 litres |
| Final gravity: | 1008 | Mash temperature: | 65ºC |
| Alcohol content: | 4.10% | Mash time: | 90 minutes |
| Bittering units: | 26 | Boil time: | 90 minutes |
| Final volume: | 23 litres | | |

In the tun
| | |
|---|---|
| Pale malt | 4220g |
| Crystal malt | 230g |
| Chocolate malt | 90g |

In the boiler
| | |
|---|---|
| Challenger (6.2%) | 52g (start of boil) |
| Fuggles hops | 10g (last 15 minutes) |
| Irish Moss | 5g (last 15 minutes) |

Malt extract version
No mash required. Replace the pale malt with 3100g of light-coloured malt extract.

59

## Tomintoul Brewery

# TOMINTOUL 80/-

| | | | |
|---|---|---|---|
| Original gravity: | 1041 | Mash liquor: | 12 litres |
| Final gravity: | 1008 | Mash temperature: | 65°C |
| Alcohol content: | 4.20% | Mash time: | 90 minutes |
| Bittering units: | 20 | Boil time: | 90 minutes |
| Final volume: | 23 litres | | |

In the tun
| | |
|---|---|
| Pale malt | 4320g |
| Crystal malt | 325g |

In the boiler
| | |
|---|---|
| Challenger (6.2%) | 40g (start of boil) |
| Goldings hops | 8g (last 15 minutes) |
| Irish Moss | 5g (last 15 minutes) |

Malt extract version
No mash required. Replace the pale malt with 3150g of light-coloured malt extract.

## Castle Eden Brewery

# CASTLE EDEN ALE

*A superb ale with a great Goldings aroma. A good balance of malt and hops creates a smooth drinkability.*

| | | | |
|---|---|---|---|
| Original gravity: | 1040 | Mash liquor: | 10 litres |
| Final gravity: | 1009 | Mash temperature: | 65ºC |
| Alcohol content: | 4.00% | Mash time: | 90 minutes |
| Bittering units: | 23 | Boil time: | 2 hours |
| Final volume: | 23 litres | | |

In the tun

| | |
|---|---|
| Pale malt | 2920g |
| Torrified wheat | 420g |

In the boiler

| | |
|---|---|
| Target hops (8.7%) | 35g (start of boil) |
| Invert sugar | 835g (after 1 hour) |
| Styrian Golding hops | 8g (last 15 minutes) |
| Irish Moss | 5g (last 15 minutes) |
| Styrian Golding hops | 7g (dry hops in cask) |

Malt extract version
Partial mash required. Replace the pale malt with 2150g of diastatic malt extract.

## Castle Eden Brewery

# WHITBREAD PORTER

*Based an old 19th century Whitbread recipe. Great tastes from the dark malts and the use of 100% Goldings create a stunning aroma and hop flavour.*

| | | | |
|---|---|---|---|
| Original gravity: | 1052 | Mash liquor: | 15 litres |
| Final gravity | 1017 | Mash temperature: | 67°C |
| Alcohol content: | 4.50% | Mash time: | 2 hours |
| Bittering units: | 36 | Boil time: | 2 hours |
| Final volume: | 23 litres | | |

In the tun

| | |
|---|---|
| Pale malt | 4555g |
| Brown malt | 1200g |
| Chocolate malt | 120g |
| Black malt | 120g |

In the boiler

| | |
|---|---|
| Goldings hops (4.0%) | 114 g (start of boil) |
| Goldings hops | 24g (last 15 minutes) |
| Irish Moss | 5g (last 15 minutes) |
| Styrian Golding hops | 10g (dry hops in cask) |

Notes:
Brown malt, although difficult to come by, is available. Whitbread no longer brew this ale at the Castle Eden brewery.

Malt extract version
Partial mash required. Replace the pale malt with 3300g of diastatic malt extract.

Castle Eden Brewery

# WINTER ROYAL

*A ruby red-coloured ale, with great character. Plenty of flavour from the malt and hops, both of which linger in the mouth*

| | | | |
|---|---|---|---|
| Original gravity: | 1054 | Mash liquor: | 15 litres |
| Final gravity: | 1011 | Mash temperature: | 66°C |
| Alcohol content: | 5.5% | Mash time: | 2 hours |
| Bittering units: | 36 | Boil time: | 2 hours |
| Final volume: | 23 litres | | |

In the tun

| | |
|---|---|
| Pale malt | 5805g |
| Crystal malt | 305g |

In the boiler

| | |
|---|---|
| Target hops (8.7%) | 52g (start of boil) |
| Styrian Golding hops | 5g (last 15 minutes) |
| Irish moss | 5g (last 15 minutes) |

Notes
Whitbread no longer brew this ale at their Castle Eden brewery.

Malt extract version
No mash required. Replace the pale malt with 4250g of light-coloured malt extract.

## Malton Brewery Co.

# MALTON PALE ALE

*The low gravity and full flavour make this an ideal session beer, which is very refreshing.*

| | | | |
|---|---|---|---|
| Original gravity: | 1034 | Mash liquor: | 10 litres |
| Final gravity: | 1009 | Mash temperature: | 65ºC |
| Alcohol content: | 3.20% | Mash time: | 90 minutes |
| Bittering units: | 30 | Boil time: | 90 minutes |
| Final volume: | 23 litres | | |

In the tun

| | |
|---|---|
| Pale malt | 3745g |
| Crystal malt | 75g |

In the boiler

| | |
|---|---|
| Challenger hops (6.2%) | 60g (start of boil) |
| Challenger hops | 12 g (last 15 minutes) |
| Irish Moss | 5g (last 15 minutes) |

Malt extract version

No mash required. Replace the pale malt with 2750g of light-coloured malt extract.

## Malton Brewery Co.

# DOUBLE CHANCE BITTER

*Malton didn't take any chances with the uncompromising bitterness of this brew, which, combined with a perfect balance of malt, make this beer a pleasure to drink*

| | | | | |
|---|---|---|---|---|
| Original gravity: | 1038 | Mash liquor: | 11 litres |
| Final gravity: | 1008 | Mash temperature: | 65ºC |
| Alcohol content: | 3.80% | Mash time: | 90 minutes |
| Bittering units: | 36 | Boil time: | 2 hours |
| Final volume: | 23 litres | | |

### In the tun

| | |
|---|---|
| Pale malt | 4185g |
| Crystal malt | 85g |

### In the boiler

| | |
|---|---|
| Challenger hops (6.2%) | 72g (start of boil) |
| Challenger hops | 20g (last 15 minutes) |
| Irish Moss | 5g (last 15 minutes) |

### Notes:

Malton brew their beers in a converted stable which was once home to the race horse *Double Chance*, winner of the Grand National in 1925, hence the name of this bitter.

### Malt extract version

No mash required. Replace the pale malt with 3050g of light-coloured malt extract.

## Malton Brewery Co.

# PICKWICK'S PORTER

*This is packed with flavour, excellent bitterness which complements the dryness of the beer well.*

| | | | |
|---|---|---|---|
| Original gravity: | 1042 | Mash liquor: | 12 litres |
| Final gravity: | 1011 | Mash temperature: | 66°C |
| Alcohol content: | 4.00% | Mash time: | 2 hours |
| Bittering units: | 42 | Boil time: | 2 hours |
| Final volume: | 23 litres | | |

### In the tun
| | |
|---|---|
| Pale malt | 3940g |
| Crystal malt | 215g |
| Black malt | 650g |

### In the boiler
| | |
|---|---|
| Challenger hops (6.2%) | 85g (start of boil) |
| Challenger hops | 17g (last 15 minutes) |
| Irish Moss | 5g (last 15 minutes) |

Malt extract version
No mash required. Replace the pale malt with 2900g of light-coloured malt extract.

## Malton Brewery Co.

# OWD BOB

*An ale with a dry fruity, character, that does not have the usual sweet edge associated with higher gravity ales. Another beer which is a pleasure to drink.*

| | | | |
|---|---|---|---|
| Original gravity: | 1055 | Mash liquor: | 16 litres |
| Final gravity: | 1009 | Mash temperature | 66°C |
| Alcohol content: | 5.90% | Mash time: | 2 hours |
| Bittering units: | 48 | Boil time: | 2 hours |
| Final volume: | 23 litres | | |

In the tun

| | |
|---|---|
| Pale malt | 5840g |
| Crystal malt | 200g |
| Black malt | 170g |

In the boiler

| | |
|---|---|
| Challenger hops (4.5%) | 97g (start of boil) |
| Challenger hops | 19g (last 15 minutes) |
| Irish Moss | 5g (last 15 minutes) |

Malt extract version
No mash required. Replace the pale malt with 4250g of light-coloured malt extract.

## Marston Moor Brewery

# CROMWELL BITTER

*A superb light, refreshing ale with a distinctive hop flavour. An excellent session beer.*

| | | | |
|---|---|---|---|
| Original gravity: | 1037 | Mash liquor: | 10 litres |
| Final gravity: | 1008 | Mash temperature: | 65°C |
| Alcohol content: | 3.70% | Mash time: | 90 minutes |
| Bittering units: | 26 | Boil time: | 90 minutes |
| Final volume: | 23 litres | | |

In the tun

| | |
|---|---|
| Pale malt | 3975g |
| Wheat malt | 105g |
| Crystal malt | 105g |

In the boiler

| | |
|---|---|
| Challenger hops (6.2%) | 52g (start of boil) |
| Styrian Golding hops | 10g (last 15 minutes) |
| Irish Moss | 5g (last 15 minutes) |

Malt extract version
Partial mash required. Replace the pale malt with 2900g of diastatic malt extract.

## Marston Moor Brewery

# BREWERS PRIDE

*A smooth, premium amber-coloured ale with a full body and a well-balanced hop flavour.*

| | | | |
|---|---|---|---|
| Original gravity: | 1042 | Mash liquor: | 12 litres |
| Final gravity: | 1009 | Mash temperature: | 65ºC |
| Alcohol content: | 4.20% | Mash time: | 90 minutes |
| Bittering units: | 32 | Boil time: | 90 minutes |
| Final volume: | 23 litres | | |

In the tun

| | |
|---|---|
| Pale malt | 4505g |
| Crystal malt | 120g |
| Wheat malt | 120g |

In the boiler

| | |
|---|---|
| Challenger hops (6.2%) | 65g (start of boil) |
| Styrian Golding hops | 13g (last 15 minutes) |
| Irish Moss | 5g (last 15 minutes) |

Malt extract version
Partial mash required. Replace the pale malt with 3300g of diastatic malt extract.

## Marston Moor Brewery

# PORTER

*Dark, ruby-coloured, stout-like ale. The use of roast barley contributes to a smooth, dry, and extremely palatable finish.*

| | | | |
|---|---|---|---|
| Original gravity: | 1042 | Mash liquor | : 12 litres |
| Final gravity: | 1009 | Mash temperature | : 66ºC |
| Alcohol content: | 4.2% | Mash time | : 2 hours |
| Bittering units: | 36 | Boil time | : 2 hours |
| Final volume: | 23 litres | | |

In the tun

| | |
|---|---|
| Pale malt | 4155g |
| Crystal malt | 120g |
| Wheat malt | 120g |
| Roast Barley | 80 g |

In the boiler

| | |
|---|---|
| Challenger hops (6.2%) | 73g (start of boil) |
| Styrian Golding hops | 15g (last 15 minutes) |
| Irish Moss | 5g (last 15 minutes) |

Malt extract version
Partial mash required. Replace the pale malt with 3050g of diastatic malt extract.

Burton Bridge Brewery

# BRIDGE BITTER

*A superb, palatable ale which has a full bodied malt appeal with ample bitterness. A good example of a premium ale.*

| | | | |
|---|---|---|---|
| Original gravity: | 1041 | Mash liquor: | 11 litres |
| Final gravity: | 1008 | Mash temperature: | 65ºC |
| Alcohol content: | 4.2% | Mash time: | 90 minutes |
| Bittering units: | 40 | Boil time: | 2 hours |
| Final volume: | 23 litres | | |

### In the tun

| | |
|---|---|
| Pale malt | 4080g |
| Crystal malt | 230g |

### In the boiler

| | |
|---|---|
| Challenger hops (6.2%) | 54g (start of boil) |
| Target hops (8.7%) | 19 g (start of boil) |
| Invert sugar | 227g (after 1 hour) |
| Challenger hops | 15g (last 15 minutes) |
| Irish Moss | 5g (last 15 minutes) |
| Styrian Golding | 5 g (dry hops in cask) |

### Malt extract version

No mash required. Replace the pale malt with 2300g of light-coloured malt extract.

## Burton Bridge Brewery

# XL

*A great tasting ale, full of flavour from the blend of malt and hops used.*

| | | | |
|---|---|---|---|
| Original gravity: | 1039 | Mash liquor: | 11 litres |
| Final gravity: | 1008 | Mash temperature: | 65°C |
| Alcohol content: | 4.0% | Mash time: | 90 minutes |
| Bittering units: | 33 | Boil time: | 90 minutes |
| Final volume: | 23 litres | | |

In the tun

| | |
|---|---|
| Pale malt | 3880g |
| Crystal malt | 215g |

In the boiler

| | |
|---|---|
| Target hops (8.7%) | 24g (start of boil) |
| Challenger hops (6.2%) | 33 g (start of boil) |
| Invert sugar | 216g (after 45 minutes) |
| Challenger hops | 11g (last 15 minutes) |
| Irish Moss | 5g (last 15 minutes) |
| Target hops | 5 g (dry hops in cask) |

Notes:

The name XL is derived from Burton's Roman past.

Malt extract version

No mash required. Replace the pale malt with 2850g of light-coloured malt extract.

## Mansfield Brewery

# RIDING BITTER

*A pale golden bitter with an aroma that jumps out of the glass to meet you!*

| | | | |
|---|---|---|---|
| Original gravity: | 1035 | Mash liquor: | 8 litres |
| Final gravity: | 1007 | Mash temperature: | 65ºC |
| Alcohol content: | 3.60% | Mash time: | 90 minutes |
| Bittering units: | 24 | Boil time: | 2 hours |
| Final volume: | 23 litres | | |

In the tun

| | |
|---|---|
| Pale malt | 2995g |

In the boiler

| | |
|---|---|
| Fuggles hops (3.3%) | 92g (start of boil) |
| Invert sugar | 658g (after 1 hour) |
| Styrian Golding hops | 18g (last 15 minutes) |
| Irish Moss | 5g (last 15 minutes) |
| Styrian Golding | 8g (dry hops in cask) |

Malt extract version
No mash required. Replace the pale malt with 2200g of light-coloured malt extract.

## Mansfield Brewery

# OLD BAILY

| | | | |
|---|---|---|---|
| Original gravity: | 1045 | Mash liquor: | 12 litres |
| Final gravity: | 1008 | Mash temperature: | 65°C |
| Alcohol content: | 4.80% | Mash time: | 90 minutes |
| Bittering units: | 30 | Boil time: | 2 hours |
| Final volume: | 23 litres | | |

In the tun

| | |
|---|---|
| Pale malt | 3850g |

In the boiler

| | |
|---|---|
| Fuggles hops (3.3%) | 114g (start of boil) |
| Invert sugar | 846g (after 1 hour) |
| Fuggles hops | 22g (last 15 minutes) |
| Irish Moss | 5g (last 15 minutes) |
| Fuggles hops | 5g (dry hops in cask) |

Malt extract version
No mash required. Replace the pale malt with 2800g of light-coloured malt extract.

Oakham Ales

# JEFFREY HUDSON BITTER

*The use of American Mount Hood hops gives this well-balanced pale beer a superb aroma.*

| | | | |
|---|---|---|---|
| Original gravity: | 1038 | Mash liquor: | 11 litres |
| Final gravity: | 1009 | Mash temperature: | 65°C |
| Alcohol content: | 3.80% | Mash time: | 90 minutes |
| Bittering units: | 33 | Boil time: | 90 minutes |
| Final volume: | 23 litres | | |

### In the tun

| | |
|---|---|
| Pale malt | 4075g |
| Wheat malt | 215g |

### In the boiler

| | |
|---|---|
| Challenger hops (6.2%) | 67g (start of boil) |
| Mount Hood hops | 13g (last 15 minutes) |
| Irish Moss | 5g (last 15 minutes) |

### Notes

The brewery was founded by John Wood, a home brewer, and although the brewery was sold in 1995, the new brewer is also a home brewer. So to savage an old saying, 'From home brewers commercial brewers grow!'.

### Malt extract version

Partial mash required. Replace the pale malt with 2300g of diastatic malt extract.

## Oakham Ales

# HUNKY DORY

*The use of amber malt adds a lovely biscuity taste to the mouthfilling presence of the pale malt and Challenger hops. A superbly well-crafted ale.*

| | | | |
|---|---|---|---|
| Original gravity: | 1044 | Mash liquor | : 12 litres |
| Final gravity: | 1009 | Mash temperature | : 65°C |
| Alcohol content: | 4.50% | Mash time | : 90 minutes |
| Bittering units: | 34 | Boil time | : 90 minutes |
| Final volume: | 23 litres | | |

### In the tun

| | |
|---|---|
| Pale malt | 4530g |
| Amber malt | 450g |

### In the boiler

| | |
|---|---|
| Challenger hops (6.2%) | 69g (start of boil) |
| Mount Hood hops | 14g (last 15 minutes) |
| Irish Moss | 5g (last 15 minutes) |

### Malt extract version

Partial mash required. Replace the pale malt with 3300g of diastatic malt extract.

## Oakham Ales

# OLD TOSSPOT

| | | | |
|---|---|---|---|
| Original gravity: | 1052 | Mash liquor: | 15 litres |
| Final gravity: | 1012 | Mash temperature: | 66ºC |
| Alcohol content: | 5.20% | Mash time: | 2 hours |
| Bittering units: | 35 | Boil time: | 2 hours |
| Final volume: | 23 litres | | |

### In the tun

| | |
|---|---|
| Pale malt | 5425g |
| Crystal malt | 465g |
| Chocolate malt | 10g |

### In the boiler

| | |
|---|---|
| Challenger hops (6.2%) | 71g (start of boil) |
| Mount Hood hops | 14g (last 15 minutes) |
| Irish Moss | 5g (last 15 minutes) |

Malt extract version
No mash required. Replace the pale malt with 3950g of light-coloured malt extract.

## Parish Brewery

# PARISH SPECIAL BITTER

*A well-balanced, copper-coloured session ale with a very pleasing hop aroma, from the use of 100% finest quality Golding hops.*

| | | | |
|---|---|---|---|
| Original gravity: | 1038 | Mash liquor: | 11 litres |
| Final gravity: | 1010 | Mash temperature: | 65ºC |
| Alcohol content: | 3.60% | Mash time: | 90 minutes |
| Bittering units: | 30 | Boil time: | 2 hours |
| Final volume: | 23 litres | | |

In the tun

| | |
|---|---|
| Pale malt | 3880g |
| Wheat malt | 215g |
| Crystal malt | 215g |

In the boiler

| | |
|---|---|
| Goldings hops (4.0%) | 94g (start of boil) |
| Goldings hops | 20g (last 15 minutes) |
| Irish Moss | 5g (last 15 minutes) |

Malt extract version
Partial mash required. Replace the pale malt with 2850g of diastatic malt extract.

## Parish Brewery

# POACHER'S ALE

| | | | |
|---|---|---|---|
| Original gravity: | 1060 | Mash liquor: | 17 litres |
| Final gravity: | 1013 | Mash temperature: | 67ºC |
| Alcohol content: | 6.00% | Mash time: | 2 hours |
| Bittering units: | 24 | Boil time: | 2 hours |
| Final volume: 23 litres | | | |

In the tun

| | |
|---|---|
| Pale malt | 5815g |
| Wheat malt | 340g |
| Crystal malt | 550g |
| Black malt | 140g |

In the boiler

| | |
|---|---|
| Goldings hops (4.0%) | 75g (start of boil) |
| Fuggles hops | 5g (last 15 minutes) |
| Irish Moss | 5g (last 15 minutes) |

Malt extract version
Partial mash required. Replace the pale malt with 4250g of diastatic malt extract.

## Springhead Brewery

# SPRINGHEAD BITTER

*A copper-coloured ale with a full malt flavour which is brilliantly offset by a lingering hop character. An easy drinking, clean tasting, hoppy session beer.*

| | | | |
|---|---|---|---|
| Original gravity: | 1040 | Mash liquor: | 11 litres |
| Final gravity: | 1009 | Mash temperature: | 65ºC |
| Alcohol content: | 4.00% | Mash time: | 90 minutes |
| Bittering units: | 23 | Boil time: | 2 hours |
| Final volume: | 23 litres | | |

In the tun
| | |
|---|---|
| Pale malt | 4445g |
| Crystal malt | 70g |

In the boiler
| | |
|---|---|
| Northdown hops (7.5%) | 38g (start of boil) |
| Northdown hops | 8g (last 15 minutes) |
| Irish Moss | 5g (last 15 minutes) |

Malt extract version
No mash required. Replace the pale malt with 3250g of light-coloured malt extract.

## Townes Brewery

# SUNSHINE

*It is unusual to find a beer brewed entirely with Bramling Cross, but what a treat when you do! The combination of pale and wheat malts with the Bramling gives a pale refreshing beer with a superb aroma .*

| | | | |
|---|---|---|---|
| Original gravity: | 1036 | Mash liquor: | 10 litres |
| Final gravity: | 1008 | Mash temperature: | 65ºC |
| Alcohol content: | 3.60% | Mash time: | 90 minutes |
| Bittering units: | 28 | Boil time: | 90 minutes |
| Final volume: | 23 litres | | |

In the tun

| | |
|---|---|
| Pale malt | 3870g |
| Wheat malt | 195g |

In the boiler

| | |
|---|---|
| Bramling Cross hops (5.5%) | 64g (start of boil) |
| Bramling Cross hops | 13g (last 15 minutes) |
| Irish Moss | 5g (last 15 minutes) |

Malt extract version

Partial mash required. Replace the pale malt with 2800g of diastatic malt extract.

## Townes Brewery

# BEST LOCKOFORD BITTER

| | | | |
|---|---|---|---|
| Original gravity: | 1040 | Mash liquor: | 11 litres |
| Final gravity: | 1010 | Mash temperature: | 66ºC |
| Alcohol content: | 4.00% | Mash time: | 90 minutes |
| Bittering units: | 33 | Boil time: | 90 minutes |
| Final volume: | 23 litres | | |

In the tun

| | |
|---|---|
| Pale malt | 4190g |
| Crystal malt | 185g |
| Wheat malt | 150g |

In the boiler

| | |
|---|---|
| Challenger hops (6.2%) | 60g (start of boil) |
| Styrian Golding (3.7%) | 11g (start of boil) |
| Styrian Golding hops | 14g (last 15 minutes) |
| Irish Moss | 5g (last 15 minutes) |

Malt extract version
Partial mash required. Replace the pale malt with 3050g of diastatic malt extract.

## Townes Brewery

# IPA

*I haven't tasted the commercial ale, but if the beer produced by this recipe is anything to go by, then I could quite happily drink this for the rest of my days. Stunning presence of hops in the mouth with just the right amount of malt make this pale ale well worth a brew*

| | | | |
|---|---|---|---|
| Original gravity: | 1045 | Mash liquor: | 13 litres |
| Final gravity: | 1010 | Mash temperature: | 65⁰C |
| Alcohol content: | 4.50% | Mash time: | 90 minutes |
| Bittering units: | 40 | Boil time: | 2 hours |
| Final volume: | 23 litres | | |

In the tun

| | |
|---|---|
| Pale malt | 4880g |
| Wheat malt | 195g |

In the boiler

| | |
|---|---|
| Willamette hops (3.7%) | 135g (start of boil) |
| Willamette hops | 27g (last 15 minutes) |
| Irish Moss | 5g (last 15 minutes) |

Malt extract version

Partial mash required. Replace the pale malt with 3550g of diastatic malt extract.

Townes Brewery

# PYNOT PORTER

*The dark malts fill your mouth with a rich taste, but balanced well with the hops. A good example of a porter.*

| | | | |
|---|---|---|---|
| Original gravity: | 1045 | Mash liquor: | 13 litres |
| Final gravity: | 1010 | Mash temperature: | 66°C |
| Alcohol content: | 4.50% | Mash time: | 2 hours |
| Bittering units: | 40 | Boil time: | 2 hours |
| Final volume: | 23 litres | | |

In the tun

| | |
|---|---|
| Pale malt | 4480g |
| Crystal malt | 155g |
| Black malt | 155g |
| Wheat Malt | 205 g |
| Roast barley | 130 g |

In the boiler

| | |
|---|---|
| Northdown hops (7.5%) | 60g (start of boil) |
| Styrian Golding hops (3.7%) | 14g (start of boil) |
| Styrian Golding hops | 15g (last 15 minutes) |
| Irish Moss | 5g (last 15 minutes) |

Malt extract version
Partial mash required. Replace the pale malt with 3300g of diastatic malt extract.

Townes Brewery

# DOUBLE DAGGER

| | | | |
|---|---|---|---|
| Original gravity | 1050 | Mash liquor: | 14 litres |
| Final gravity: | 1011 | Mash temperature: | 65ºC |
| Alcohol content: | 5.00% | Mash time: | 90 minutes |
| Bittering units: | 44 | Boil time: | 2 hours |
| Final volume: | 23 litres | | |

### In the tun

| | |
|---|---|
| Pale malt | 5185g |
| Crystal malt | 200g |
| Wheat malt | 200g |
| Black malt | 85g |

### In the boiler

| | |
|---|---|
| Northdown hops (7.5%) | 49g (start of boil) |
| Willamette hops (3.7%) | 49g (start of boil) |
| Willamette hops | 20g (last 15 minutes) |
| Irish Moss | 5g (last 15 minutes) |

Malt extract version
Partial mash required. Replace the pale malt with 3800g of diastatic malt extract.

## Crouch Vale Brewery

# BEST DARK ALE

*A pleasant mild, with a higher than average bitterness.*

| | | | |
|---|---|---|---|
| Original gravity: | 1036 | Mash liquor: | 10 litres |
| Final gravity: | 1009 | Mash temperature: | 64ºC |
| Alcohol content: | 3.50% | Mash time: | 90 minutes |
| Bittering units: | 30 | Boil time: | 90 minutes |
| Final volume | 23 litres | | |

### In the tun

| | |
|---|---|
| Mild ale malt | 3870g |
| Roast barley | 205g |

### In the boiler

| | |
|---|---|
| Challenger hops (6.2%) | 60g (start of boil) |
| Goldings hops | 10g (last 15 minutes) |
| Irish Moss | 5g (last 15 minutes) |

Malt extract version
No mash required. Replace the mild ale malt with 2800g of light-coloured malt extract.

## Crouch Vale Brewery

# WOODHAM IPA BITTER

*A superbly well-balanced beer, which has a great hop character.*

| | | | |
|---|---|---|---|
| Original gravity: | 1036 | Mash liquor: | 10 litres |
| Final gravity: | 1009 | Mash temperature: | 65ºC |
| Alcohol content: | 3.50% | Mash time: | 90 minutes |
| Bittering units: | 32 | Boil time: | 2 hours |
| Final volume: | 23 litres | | |

In the tun

| | |
|---|---|
| Pale malt | 3870g |
| Crystal malt | 205g |

In the boiler

| | |
|---|---|
| Challenger hops (6.2%) | 65g (start of boil) |
| Goldings hops | 12g (last 15 minutes) |
| Irish Moss | 5g (last 15 minutes) |
| Goldings hops | 5g (dry hops in cask) |

Malt extract version
No mash required. Replace the pale malt with 2800g of light-coloured malt extract.

## Crouch Vale Brewery

# BEST BITTER

*Another of those beers you could quite happily drink all night, a stunning level of bitterness with a fine malt flavour makes this reddy coloured ale a pleasure to drink.*

| | | | |
|---|---|---|---|
| Original gravity: | 1038 | Mash liquor: | 11 litres |
| Final gravity: | 1007 | Mash temperature: | 65°C |
| Alcohol content: | 4.00% | Mash time: | 90 minutes |
| Bittering units: | 35 | Boil time: | 2 hours |
| Final volume: | 23 litres | | |

In the tun

| | |
|---|---|
| Pale malt | 4000g |
| Crystal malt | 305g |

In the boiler

| | |
|---|---|
| Challenger hops (6.2%) | 72g (start of boil) |
| Goldings hops | 14g (last 15 minutes) |
| Irish Moss | 5g (last 15 minutes) |
| Goldings hops | 8g (dry hops in cask) |

Malt extract version
No mash required. Replace the pale malt with 2900g of light-coloured malt extract.

## Crouch Vale Brewery

# MILLENNIUM GOLD

*A full flavoured, golden coloured beer.*

| | | | |
|---|---|---|---|
| Original gravity: | 1042 | Mash liquor: | 12 litres |
| Final gravity: | 1009 | Mash temperature: | 65⁰C |
| Alcohol content: | 4.2% | Mash time: | 90 minutes |
| Bittering units: | 35 | Boil time: | 2 hours |
| Final volume: | 23 litres | | |

In the tun

| | |
|---|---|
| Pale malt | 4730g |

In the boiler

| | |
|---|---|
| Challenger hops (6.2%) | 72g (start of boil) |
| Goldings hops | 14g (last 15 minutes) |
| Irish Moss | 5g (last 15 minutes) |
| Goldings hops | 10g (dry hops in cask) |

Malt extract version
No mash required. Replace the pale malt with 3450g of light-coloured malt extract.

## Crouch Vale Brewery

# STRONG ANGLIAN SPECIAL (aka SAS)

*Drink with care … this beer drinks easier than its gravity would suggest, and its delicious flavour begs another glass. Perhaps the abbreviation SAS doesn't come from the beer's full name, but from the regiment – elite and silently creeps up on you.*

| | | | |
|---|---|---|---|
| Original gravity: | 1048 | Mash liquor: | 14 litres |
| Final gravity: | 1009 | Mash temperature: | 660C |
| Alcohol content: | 5.00% | Mash time: | 2 hours |
| Bittering units: | 37 | Boil time: | 2 hours |
| Final volume: | 23 litres | | |

In the tun

| | |
|---|---|
| Pale malt | 5110g |
| Crystal malt | 325g |

In the boiler

| | |
|---|---|
| Challenger hops (6.2%) | 75g (start of boil) |
| Goldings hops | 15g (last 15 minutes) |
| Irish Moss | 5g (last 15 minutes) |
| Goldings hops | 8g (dry hops in cask) |

Malt extract version
No mash required. Replace the pale malt with 3750g of light-coloured malt extract.

## Crouch Vale Brewery

# SANTA'S REVENGE

| | | | |
|---|---|---|---|
| Original gravity: | 1058 | Mash liquor: | 12 litres |
| Final gravity: | 1013 | Mash temperature: | 66°C |
| Alcohol content: | 5.80% | Mash time: | 2 hours |
| Bittering units: | 37 | Boil time: | 2 hours |
| Final volume: | 23 litres | | |

### In the tun
| | |
|---|---|
| Pale malt | 4525g |
| Crystal malt | 305g |

### In the boiler
| | |
|---|---|
| Challenger hops (6.2%) | 75g (start of boil) |
| Invert sugar | 1207g (after 1 hour) |
| Goldings hops | 15g (last 15 minutes) |
| Irish Moss | 5g (last 15 minutes) |
| Goldings hops | 5 g (dry hops in cask) |

### Malt extract version
No mash required. Replace the pale malt with 3300g of light-coloured malt extract.

## Crouch Vale Brewery

# WILLIE WARMER

*A sweetish brew which is countered by the hops and roast barley. This is strong and I would suggest savouring it by the nip bottle instead of pints.*

| | | | |
|---|---|---|---|
| Original gravity: | 1060 | Mash liquor: | 12 litres |
| Final gravity: | 1010 | Mash temperature: | 66ºC |
| Alcohol content: | 6.50% | Mash time: | 2 hours |
| Bittering units: | 40 | Boil time: | 2 hours |
| Final volume: | 23 litres | | |

In the tun

| | |
|---|---|
| Pale malt | 4280g |
| Roast barley | 305g |

In the boiler

| | |
|---|---|
| Challenger hops (6.2%) | 82g (start of boil) |
| Invert sugar | 1529g (after 1 hour) |
| Goldings hops | 16g (last 15 minutes) |
| Irish Moss | 5g (last 15 minutes) |
| Goldings hops | 8g (dry hops in cask) |

Malt extract version

No mash required. Replace the pale malt with 3100g of light-coloured malt extract.

## McMullen & Sons

# ORIGINAL AK

*A beer which is stronger than the gravity suggests. An easily drinkable ale with a light, but pleasant hop flavour.*

| | | | |
|---|---|---|---|
| Original gravity: | 1033 | Mash liquor: | 9 litres |
| Final gravity: | 1004 | Mash temperature: | 630C |
| Alcohol content: | 3.70% | Mash time: | 90 minutes |
| Bittering units: | 22 | Boil time: | 90 minutes |
| Final volume: | 23 litres | | |

In the tun

| | |
|---|---|
| Pale malt | 2835g |
| Chocolate malt | 35g |
| Flaked maize | 215g |

In the boiler

| | |
|---|---|
| WGV hops (4.5%) | 61g (start of boil) |
| Maltose syrup | 461g (after 45 minutes) |
| WGV hops | 12g (last 15 minutes) |
| Irish Moss | 5g (last 15 minutes) |

Malt extract version
Partial mash required. Replace the pale malt with 2100g of diastatic malt extract.

## McMullen & Sons

# COUNTRY BEST BITTER

*One of my favourite ales from a favourite brewery. A superb balance of malt to hops creates a bitter that is not only pleasing to drink but leaves you wanting another. This used to be served to perfection in a country pub called The Woodsman, just outside Broxbourne, Herts*

| | | | |
|---|---|---|---|
| Original gravity: | 1041 | Mash liquor: | 11 litres |
| Final gravity: | 1008 | Mash temperature: | 65°C |
| Alcohol content: | 4.20% | Mash time: | 90 minutes |
| Bittering units: | 30 | Boil time: | 90 minutes |
| Final volume: | 23 litres | | |

In the tun

| | |
|---|---|
| Pale malt | 3340g |
| Crystal malt | 175g |
| Flaked maize | 265g |

In the boiler

| | |
|---|---|
| Progress hops (5.5%) | 68g (start of boil) |
| Maltose syrup | 616g (after 45 minutes) |
| Progress hops | 14g (last 15 minutes) |
| Irish Moss | 5g (last 15 minutes) |

Notes:

Tony Skipper, McMullen's head brewer and production director, was named Brewer of the Year in 1995. McMullen now produce a new ale, Harvest Moon, which is available from larger Tesco stores.

Malt extract version

Partial mash required. Replace the pale malt with 2450g of diastatic malt extract.

## McMullen & Sons

# STRONGHART

*A malty full drinking ale, with an excellent balance of hops.*

| | | | |
|---|---|---|---|
| Original gravity: | 1070 | Mash liquor: | 19 litres |
| Final gravity: | 1016 | Mash temperature: | 67°C |
| Alcohol content: | 7.00% | Mash time: | 2 hours |
| Bittering units: | 33 | Boil time: | 2 hours |
| Final volume: | 23 litres | | |

In the tun

| | |
|---|---|
| Pale malt | 5490g |
| Crystal malt | 300g |
| Flaked maize | 300g |

In the boiler

| | |
|---|---|
| WGV hops (4.5%) | 88g (start of boil) |
| Maltose syrup | 1335g (after 1 hour) |
| WGV hops | 18g (last 15 minutes) |
| Irish Moss | 5g (last 15 minutes) |

Malt extract version
Partial mash required. Replace the pale malt with 4010g of diastatic (DMS) malt extract.

## Poole Brewery

# DOLPHIN BITTER

| | | | |
|---|---|---|---|
| Original gravity: | 1038 | Mash liquor: | 11 litres |
| Final gravity: | 1009 | Mash temperature: | 65ºC |
| Alcohol content: | 3.80% | Mash time: | 90 minutes |
| Bittering units: | 35 | Boil time: | 2 hours |
| Final volume: | 23 litres | | |

In the tun

| | |
|---|---|
| Pale malt | 3785g |
| Crystal malt | 540g |

In the boiler

| | |
|---|---|
| Fuggles hops (3.3%) | 133g (start of boil) |
| Goldings hops | 27g (last 15 minutes) |
| Irish Moss | 5g (last 15 minutes) |

Malt extract version
No mash required. Replace the pale malt with 2750g of light-coloured malt extract.

## Poole Brewery

# BOSUN BEST BITTER

*Extremely popular with local mashers, "Great malt taste but what a fantastic hoppiness and aroma" was one of the comments received. Well worth a brew.*

| | | | |
|---|---|---|---|
| Original gravity: | 1047 | Mash liquor: | 13 litres |
| Final gravity: | 1011 | Mash temperature: | 65°C |
| Alcohol content: | 4.60% | Mash time: | 90 minutes |
| Bittering units: | 40 | Boil time: | 2 hours |
| Final volume: | 23 litres | | |

In the tun
| | |
|---|---|
| Pale malt | 4925g |
| Crystal malt | 400g |

In the boiler
| | |
|---|---|
| Goldings hops (4.0%) | 125g (start of boil) |
| Goldings hops | 25g (last 15 minutes) |
| Irish Moss | 5g (last 15 minutes) |
| Goldings hops | 25g (dry hops in cask) |

Notes:
The dry hop quantity is correct, commercially the brewery uses approx. 225g of hops per brewer's barrel giving a huge Goldings aroma.

Malt extract version
No mash required. Replace the pale malt with 3600g of light-coloured malt extract.

## Ushers of Trowbridge

# BEST BITTER

*Another personal favourite, a quality session bitter which is bright and smooth with the full taste of hops and barley. A well-balanced ale with a clean finish. At the 1996 Burton Beer Festival the draught can version of this ale won a silver medal.*

| | | | |
|---|---|---|---|
| Original gravity: | 1037 | Mash liquor: | 10 litres |
| Final gravity: | 1008 | Mash temperature: | 65ºC |
| Alcohol content: | 3.80% | Mash time: | 90 minutes |
| Bittering units: | 27 | Boil time: | 2 hours |
| Final volume: | 23 litres | | |

In the tun

| | |
|---|---|
| Pale malt | 4015g |
| Crystal malt | 170g |

In the boiler

| | |
|---|---|
| Target hops (8.7%) | 39g (start of boil) |
| Styrian Golding hops | 8g (last 15 minutes) |
| Irish Moss | 5g (last 15 minutes) |
| Styrian Golding hops | 5g (dry hops in cask) |

Notes:
Ushers add the target hops in pellet form

Malt extract version
No mash required. Replace the pale malt with 2950g of light-coloured malt extract.

# Ushers of Trowbridge

## FOUNDERS ALE

*An extra special bitter with a rich floral hop aroma. The palate is full bodied with citrus hop notes, adding to the beer's fruity and warming character.*

| | | | |
|---|---|---|---|
| Original gravity: | 1045 | Mash liquor: | 13 litres |
| Final gravity: | 1010 | Mash temperature: | 65ºC |
| Alcohol content: | 4.50% | Mash time: | 90 minutes |
| Bittering units: | 34 | Boil time: | 2 hours |
| Final volume: | 23 litres | | |

### In the tun

| | |
|---|---|
| Pale malt | 4745g |
| Crystal malt | 360g |

### In the boiler

| | |
|---|---|
| Target hops (8.7%) | 49g (start of boil) |
| Styrian Golding hops | 10g (last 15 minutes) |
| Irish Moss | 5g (last 15 minutes) |
| Styrian Golding hops | 10 g (dry hops in cask) |

Malt extract version
No mash required. Replace the pale malt with 3450g of light-coloured malt extract.

## Ushers of Trowbridge

# 1824 PARTICULAR

*Dark ruby ale, a truly warming brew for the winter months! Pleasant floral hop aroma with a fruity and nutty palate, a long hoppy finish with fruity notes.*

| | | | |
|---|---|---|---|
| Original gravity: | 1060 | Mash liquor: | 17 litres |
| Final gravity: | 1012 | Mash temperature: | 660C |
| Alcohol content: | 6.20% | Mash time: | 2 hours |
| Bittering units: | 33 | Boil time: | 2 hours |
| Final volume: | 23 litres | | |

In the tun
| | |
|---|---|
| Pale malt | 6265g |
| Crystal malt | 545g |

In the boiler
| | |
|---|---|
| Target hops (8.7%) | 48g (start of boil) |
| Styrian Golding hops | 10g (last 15 minutes) |
| Irish Moss | 5g (last 15 minutes) |

Malt extract version
No mash required. Replace the pale malt with 4600g of light-coloured malt extract.

## Wadworth & Co.

# HENRY WADWORTH IPA

| | | | |
|---|---|---|---|
| Original gravity: | 1034 | Mash liquor: | 10 litres |
| Final gravity: | 1005 | Mash temperature: | 65°C |
| Alcohol content: | 3.80% | Mash time: | 90 minutes |
| Bittering units: | 22 | Boil time: | 90 minutes |
| Final volume: | 23 litres | | |

In the tun

| | |
|---|---|
| Pale malt | 3580g |
| Crystal malt | 150g |

In the boiler

| | |
|---|---|
| Fuggles hops (3.3%) | 83g (start of boil) |
| Invert sugar | 76g (after 45 minutes) |
| Goldings hops | 17g (last 15 minutes) |
| Irish Moss | 5g (last 15 minutes) |

Malt extract version
No mash required. Replace the pale malt with 2600g of light-coloured malt extract.

## Wadworth & Co.

# 6X

*A fine premium, copper-coloured beer with plenty of flavour.*

| | | | |
|---|---|---|---|
| Original gravity: | 1040 | Mash liquor: | 11 litres |
| Final gravity: | 1007 | Mash temperature: | 650C |
| Alcohol content: | 4.30% | Mash time: | 90 minutes |
| Bittering units: | 22 | Boil time: | 2 hours |
| Final volume: | 23 litres | | |

In the tun

| | |
|---|---|
| Pale malt | 3945g |
| Crystal malt | 180g |

In the boiler

| | |
|---|---|
| Fuggles hops (3.3%) | 84g (start of boil) |
| Invert sugar | 307g (after 1 hour) |
| Goldings hops | 17g (last 15 minutes) |
| Irish Moss | 5g (last 15 minutes) |

Malt extract version
No mash required. Replace the pale malt with 2900g of light-coloured malt extract.

# Wadworth & Co.

## OLD TIMER

| | | | |
|---|---|---|---|
| Original gravity: | 1055 | Mash liquor: | 15 litres |
| Final gravity: | 1010 | Mash temperature: | 66°C |
| Alcohol content: | 5.80% | Mash time: | 2 hours |
| Bittering units: | 22 | Boil time: | 2 hours |
| Final volume: | 23 litres | | |

In the tun

| | |
|---|---|
| Pale malt | 5425g |
| Crystal malt | 180g |

In the boiler

| | |
|---|---|
| Fuggles hops (3.3%) | 83g (start of boil) |
| Invert sugar | 422g (after 1 hour) |
| Goldings hops | 17g (last 15 minutes) |
| Irish Moss | 5g (last 15 minutes) |

Malt extract version
No mash required. Replace the pale malt with 3950g of light-coloured malt extract.

## Whitbread (Flowers Brewery)

# WEST COUNTRY PALE ALE

*This ale's low gravity makes it an ideal session beer.*

| | | | |
|---|---|---|---|
| Original gravity: | 1031 | Mash liquor: | 9 litres |
| Final gravity: | 1007 | Mash temperature: | 650C |
| Alcohol content: | 3.00% | Mash time: | 90 minutes |
| Bittering units: | 25 | Boil time: | 90 minutes |
| Final volume: | 23 litres | | |
| In the tun | | | |

In the tun
| | |
|---|---|
| Pale malt | 3305g |
| Crystal malt | 140g |

In the boiler
| | |
|---|---|
| Target hops (8.7%) | 31g (start of boil) |
| WGV hops (4.5%) | 10g (start of boil) |
| Styrian Golding hops | 8g (last 15 minutes) |
| Irish Moss | 5g (last 15 minutes) |
| Golding hops | 5 g (dry hops in cask) |

Notes
The Target hops replace the hop extract which is used commercially.

Malt extract version
No mash required. Replace the pale malt with 2400g of light-coloured malt extract.

Whitbread (Flowers Brewery)

# FREMLINS BITTER

| | | | |
|---|---|---|---|
| Original gravity: | 1036 | Mash liquor: | 10 litres |
| Final gravity: | 1008 | Mash temperature: | 65ºC |
| Alcohol content: | 3.50% | Mash time: | 90 minutes |
| Bittering units: | 24 | Boil time: | 90 minutes |
| Final volume: | 23 litres | | |

### In the tun

| | |
|---|---|
| Pale malt | 2685g |
| Crystal malt | 190g |
| Torrified wheat | 460g |

### In the boiler

| | |
|---|---|
| Target hops (8.7%) | 34g (start of boil) |
| Invert sugar | 498g (after 45 minutes) |
| Styrian Golding hops | 7g (last 15 minutes) |
| Irish Moss | 5g (last 15 minutes) |
| Styrian Golding hops | 5g (dry hops in cask) |

### Notes
The Target hops replace the hop extract which is used commercially.

### Malt extract version
Partial mash required. Replace the pale malt with 1950g of diastatic malt extract.

## Whitbread (Flowers Brewery)

# WHITBREAD BEST BITTER

| | | | |
|---|---|---|---|
| Original gravity: | 1036 | Mash liquor: | 10 litres |
| Final gravity: | 1008 | Mash temperature: | 65°C |
| Alcohol content: | 3.60% | Mash time: | 90 minutes |
| Bittering units: | 26 | Boil time: | 90 minutes |
| Final volume: | 23 litres | | |

### In the tun

| | |
|---|---|
| Pale malt | 3900g |
| Crystal malt | 165g |

### In the boiler

| | |
|---|---|
| WGV hops (4.5%) | 7g (start of boil) |
| Target hops (8.7%) | 32g (start of boil) |
| Styrian Golding hops (3.7%) | 4g (start of boil) |
| Styrian Golding hops | 9g (last 15 minutes) |
| Irish Moss | 5g (last 15 minutes) |
| Styrian Golding hops | 2 g (dry cask in hops) |

### Notes

The Target hops replace the hop extract which is used commercially.

### Malt extract version

No mash required. Replace the pale malt with 2850g of light-coloured malt extract.

## Whitbread (Flowers Brewery)

# FLOWERS IPA

*This is one of those beers that is immensely enjoyable to drink, with a pleasing balance of malt and hops.*

| | | | |
|---|---|---|---|
| Original gravity: | 1036 | Mash liquor: | 9 litres |
| Final gravity: | 1008 | Mash temperature: | 650C |
| Alcohol content: | 3.60% | Mash time: | 90 minutes |
| Bittering units: | 24 | Boil time: | 2 hours |
| Final volume: | 23 litres | | |

### In the tun

| | |
|---|---|
| Pale malt | 3095g |
| Crystal malt | 290g |

### In the boiler

| | |
|---|---|
| Target hops (8.7%) | 39g (start of boil) |
| Styrian Golding hops (3.7%) | 8g (start of boil) |
| Invert sugar | 484g (after 1 hour) |
| Styrian Golding hops | 8g (last 15 minutes) |
| Irish Moss | 5g (last 15 minutes) |
| Target hops | 5 g (dry hops in cask) |

### Malt extract version

No mash required. Replace the pale malt with 2250g of light-coloured malt extract.

## Whitbread (Flowers Brewery)

# FLOWERS ORIGINAL BITTER

*As this is a firm favourite with my wife, family and friends, this recipe has probably had more test brews than any other! A strong cask ale, chestnut in colour with a distinctive fruity hop aroma and taste. Full malt flavour with a dry hop finish and some raisin and sultana notes.*

| | | | |
|---|---|---|---|
| Original gravity: | 1044 | Mash liquor: | 12 litres |
| Final gravity: | 1009 | Mash temperature: | 650C |
| Alcohol content: | 4.50% | Mash time: | 90 minutes |
| Bittering units: | 30 | Boil time: | 2 hours |
| Final volume: | 23 litres | | |

108

In the tun

| | |
|---|---|
| Pale malt | 3785g |
| Crystal malt | 355g |

In the boiler

| | |
|---|---|
| Target hops (8.7%) | 39g (start of boil) |
| Styrian Golding hops (3.7%) | 10g (start of boil) |
| Invert sugar | 591g (after 1 hour) |
| Styrian Golding hops | 10g (last 15 minutes) |
| Irish Moss | 5g (last 15 minutes) |
| Styrian Golding hops | 5g (dry hops in cask) |
| Target hops | 2g (dry hops in cask) |

Notes:
Whitbread use a blend of Target hop oil and Styrian whole hops for aroma. For test brews I used Brupaks' grains and hops and a Gervin No. 1 English Ale yeast.

Malt extract version
No mash required. Replace the pale malt with 2750g of light-coloured malt extract.

## Mildmay Brewery

# COLOURS BEST BITTER

*An example of how good bitters can be. The hop character initially fills your mouth, followed by a full-bodied maltiness. Excellent aroma.*

| | | | |
|---|---|---|---|
| Original gravity: | 1040 | Mash liquor | : 11 litres |
| Final gravity: | 1011 | Mash temperature | : 65ºC |
| Alcohol content: | 3.80% | Mash time | : 90 minutes |
| Bittering units: | 34 | Boil time | : 90 minutes |
| Final volume: | 23 litres | | |

### In the tun
| | |
|---|---|
| Pale malt | 4130g |
| Crystal malt | 230g |
| Wheat flour | 70g |
| Flaked barley | 115g |

### In the boiler
| | |
|---|---|
| Target hops (8.7%) | 44g (start of boil) |
| Styrian Golding hops (3.7%) | 11g (start of boil) |
| Styrian Golding hops | 11g (last 15 minutes) |
| Irish Moss | 5g (last 15 minutes) |
| Styrian Golding | 5g (dry hops in cask) |

Notes:
Mildmay used to use dry hops. If you are interested in adding hops to the cask, then only add 12g of Styrian Golding in the last 15 minutes and add 8g to the cask.

Malt extract version
Partial mash required. Replace the pale malt with 3000g of diastatic malt extract.

## Mildmay Brewery

# OLD HORSE WHIP

*I only came across one other brewery using 100% Saaz hops in an ale and that was Harviestoun (Scotland). The use of Saaz adds a stunning aroma and hop flavour to this immensely smooth drinking strong pale ale.*

| | | | |
|---|---|---|---|
| Original gravity: | 1054 | Mash liquor: | 15 litres |
| Final gravity: | 1010 | Mash temperature: | 65°C |
| Alcohol content: | 5.7% | Mash time: | 2 hours |
| Bittering units: | 38 | Boil time: | 2 hours |
| Final volume: | 23 litres | | |

In the tun

| | |
|---|---|
| Pale malt | 5970g |
| Flaked barley | 120g |

In the boiler

| | |
|---|---|
| Saaz hops (1.5%) | 317g (start of boil) |
| Saaz hops | 63g (last 15 minutes) |
| Irish Moss | 5g (last 15 minutes) |

Notes:
Saaz had a particularly low acid when the recipe was formulated. Check what acid is currently available and, if necessary, recalculate hop weight. This ale is available on draught and in bottles.

Malt extract version
Partial mash required. Replace the pale malt with 4350g of diastatic malt extract.

## J W Lees & Company

# LEES BITTER

| | | | |
|---|---|---|---|
| Original gravity: | 1038 | Mash liquor: | 11 litres |
| Final gravity: | 1007 | Mash temperature: | 65⁰C |
| Alcohol content: | 4.00% | Mash time: | 90 minutes |
| Bittering units: | 28 | Boil time: | 90 minutes |
| Final volume: | 23 litres | | |

### In the tun
Pale malt            4255g

### In the boiler
| | |
|---|---|
| Goldings hops (4.0%) | 88g (start of boil) |
| Goldings hops | 18g (last 15 minutes) |
| Irish Moss | 5g (last 15 minutes) |

### Malt extract version
No mash required. Replace the pale malt with 3100g of light-coloured malt extract.

## J W Lees & Company

# MOONRAKER

| | | | |
|---|---|---|---|
| Original gravity: | 1073 | Mash liquor: | 20 litres |
| Final gravity: | 1015 | Mash temperature: | 67°C |
| Alcohol content: | 7.5% | Mash time: | 2 hours |
| Bittering units: | 30 | Boil time: | 2 hours |
| Final volume: | 23 litres | | |

In the tun

| | |
|---|---|
| Pale malt | 8215g |

In the boiler

| | |
|---|---|
| Goldings hops (4.0%) | 94g (start of boil) |
| Goldings hops | 19g (last 15 minutes) |
| Irish Moss | 5g (last 15 minutes) |

Malt extract version

No mash required. Replace the pale malt with 6000g of light-coloured malt extract.

# Other recipes

Although all the recipes in this book are based on commercial beers that I have admired and enjoyed, not every brewery, whether large or small, looks for the publicity that a book of this type freely offers. Perhaps they are frightened of the opposition from home brewers!

Whatever their reasons, for copyright purposes their wishes must be obeyed. So the recipes in the following section are attributable to me alone. You might enjoy making them and trying to decide what the equivalent commercial beer is – but please don't ask if you are right! But in any case, I am sure that you will enjoy them.

# Bitters and pale ales

## 100% SATISFACTION

*The use of just pale malt and traditional Goldings hops produces a pale beer, with a good body, pleasing aroma, and quite a hoppy finish. Your thirst will be 100% satisfied with this brew. A well-crafted pale beer.*

| | | | |
|---|---|---|---|
| Original gravity: | 1040 | Mash liquor: | 11 litres |
| Final gravity: | 1009 | Mash temperature: | 65°C |
| Alcohol content: | 4.00% | Mash time: | 90 minutes |
| Bittering units: | 24 | Boil time: | 90 minutes |
| Final volume: | 23 litres | | |

In the tun
Pale malt                4500g

In the boiler
Goldings hops (4.0%)     75g (start of boil)
Goldings hops            15g (last 15 minutes)
Irish Moss               5g (last 15 minutes)

Malt extract version
No mash required. Replace the pale malt with 3300g of light-coloured malt extract.

# AMBER GAMBLER

*A dark amber ale, with a mouth-filling full bodied malt character.*

| | | | |
|---|---|---|---|
| Original gravity: | 1042 | Mash liquor: | 12 litres |
| Final gravity: | 1008 | Mash temperature: | 660C |
| Alcohol content: | 4.4% | Mash time: | 90 minutes |
| Bittering units: | 40 | Boil time | 2 hours |
| Final volume: | 23 litres | | |

In the tun

| | |
|---|---|
| Pale malt | 4440g |
| Crystal malt | 285g |
| Roast Barley | 35g |

In the boiler

| | |
|---|---|
| Northdown hops (7.5%) | 67g (start of boil) |
| Northdown hops | 10g (last 15 minutes) |
| Irish Moss | 5g (last 15 minutes) |

Malt extract version
No mash required. Replace the pale malt with 3250g of light-coloured malt extract.

## ANOTHER PINT

*An ale with a full body, and an exceptional malt and hop appeal. Once tasted you'll definitely be wanting Another Pint!*

| | | | |
|---|---|---|---|
| Original gravity: | 1052 | Mash liquor: | 15 litres |
| Final gravity: | 1010 | Mash temperature: | 650C |
| Alcohol content: | 5.40% | Mash time: | 2 hours |
| Bittering units: | 43 | Boil time: | 2 hours |
| Final volume: | 23 litres | | |

In the tun

| | |
|---|---|
| Pale malt | 4275g |
| Crystal malt | 380g |
| Wheat malt | 145g |
| Amber malt | 290g |
| Torrified wheat | 380g |

In the boiler

| | |
|---|---|
| Target hops (8.7%) | 31g (start of boil) |
| Omega hops (8.5%) | 32g (start of boil) |
| Maltose syrup | 349g (after 1 hour) |
| Goldings hops | 13 g (last 15 minutes) |
| Irish Moss | 5g (last 15 minutes) |
| Goldings hops | 5 g (dry hops in cask) |

Notes:
Substitute Omega with 31g of Challenger (6.2%) if unavailable.

Malt extract version
Partial mash required. Replace the pale malt with 3100g of diastatic malt extract.

# BITTER BITTER

*So good that we named it twice! A breathtaking level of bitterness, countered by a full-bodied maltiness.*

| | | | |
|---|---|---|---|
| Original gravity: | 1040 | Mash liquor: | 11 litres |
| Final gravity: | 1007 | Mash temperature: | 65ºC |
| Alcohol content: | 4.20% | Mash time: | 90 minutes |
| Bittering units: | 35 | Boil time: | 90 minutes |
| Final volume: | 23 litres | | |

In the tun

| | |
|---|---|
| Pale malt | 3865g |
| Crystal malt | 230g |
| Wheat malt | 455g |

In the boiler

| | |
|---|---|
| Challenger hops (6.2%) | 71g (start of boil) |
| Challenger hops | 14g (last 15 minutes) |
| Irish Moss | 5g (last 15 minutes) |

Malt extract version
Partial mash required. Replace the pale malt with 2800g of diastatic malt extract.

## BOROUGH BITTER

*An easy-drinking session bitter.*

| | | | |
|---|---|---|---|
| Original gravity: | 1036 | Mash liquor: | 10 litres |
| Final gravity: | 1007 | Mash temperature: | 65ºC |
| Alcohol content: | 3.70% | Mash time: | 90 minutes |
| Bittering units: | 26 | Boil time: | 2 hours |
| Final volume: | 23 litres | | |

In the tun

| | |
|---|---|
| Pale malt | 3490g |
| Crystal malt | 330g |
| Torrified wheat | 290g |

In the boiler

| | |
|---|---|
| Challenger hops (6.2%) | 52g (start of boil) |
| Goldings hops | 10g (last 15 minutes) |
| Irish Moss | 5g (last 15 minutes) |

Malt extract version
Partial mash required. Replace the pale malt with 2550g of diastatic malt extract.

# BBB – BRIDGEND BEST BITTER

*A pleasing balance of malt and hops makes this copper-coloured ale a pleasure to drink.*

| | | | |
|---|---|---|---|
| Original gravity: | 1046 | Mash liquor: | 13 litres |
| Final gravity: | 1010 | Mash temperature: | 65°C |
| Alcohol content: | 4.60% | Mash time: | 90 minutes |
| Bittering units: | 34 | Boil time: | 2 hours |
| Final volume: | 23 litres | | |

In the tun

| | |
|---|---|
| Pale malt | 3835g |
| Crystal malt | 245g |

In the boiler

| | |
|---|---|
| Challenger hops (6.2%) | 65g (start of boil) |
| Challenger hops | 10g (last 15 minutes) |
| Irish Moss | 5g (last 15 minutes) |

Malt extract version
No mash required. Replace the pale malt with 3600g of light-coloured malt extract.

## BSA – BRIDGEND STRONG ALE

*A full bodied amber ale with a kick to it.*

| | | | |
|---|---|---|---|
| Original gravity: | 1046 | Mash liquor: | 13 litres |
| Final gravity: | 1010 | Mash temperature: | 65°C |
| Alcohol content: | 4.60% | Mash time: | 90 minutes |
| Bittering units: | 34 | Boil time: | 2 hours |
| Final volume: | 23 litres | | |

In the tun

| | |
|---|---|
| Pale malt | 4945g |
| Crystal malt | 260g |

In the boiler

| | |
|---|---|
| Challenger hops (6.2%) | 69g (start of boil) |
| Challenger hops | 10g (last 15 minutes) |
| Irish Moss | 5g (last 15 minutes) |

Malt extract version
No mash required. Replace the pale malt with 3600g of light-coloured malt extract.

# COITY BEST BITTER

*A lightly hopped, sweet-edged bitter.*

| | | | |
|---|---|---|---|
| Original gravity: | 1036 | Mash liquor: | 8 litres |
| Final gravity: | 1009 | Mash temperature: | 65°C |
| Alcohol content: | 3.50% | Mash time: | 90 minutes |
| Bittering units: | 24 | Boil time: | 2 hours |
| Final volume: | 23 litres | | |

In the tun

| | |
|---|---|
| Pale malt | 3125g |

In the boiler

| | |
|---|---|
| WGV hops (4.5%) | 67g (start of boil) |
| Maltose syrup | 686g (after 1 hour) |
| Fuggles hops | 14g (last 15 minutes) |
| Irish Moss | 5g (last 15 minutes) |

Malt extract version
No mash required. Replace the pale malt with 2300g of light-coloured malt extract.

## COLLIER BITTER

*A sweetish brew which is excellently balanced with a fine hop flavour.*

| | | | |
|---|---|---|---|
| Original gravity: | 1040 | Mash liquor: | 11 litres |
| Final gravity: | 1009 | Mash temperature: | 65°C |
| Alcohol content: | 4.00% | Mash time: | 90 minutes |
| Bittering units: | 30 | Boil time: | 90 minutes |
| Final volume: | 23 litres | | |

In the tun

| | |
|---|---|
| Pale malt | 3870g |
| Crystal malt | 230g |
| Wheat malt | 455g |

In the boiler

| | |
|---|---|
| Challenger hops (6.2%) | 60g (start of boil) |
| Fuggles hops | 12g (last 15 minutes) |
| Irish Moss | 5g (last 15 minutes) |

Malt extract version

Partial mash required. Replace the pale malt with 2800g of diastatic malt extract.

# COUNTRYWIDE LIGHT ALE

*Its low alcohol content makes this an ideal session beer.*

| | | | |
|---|---|---|---|
| Original gravity: | 1032 | Mash liquor: | 8 litres |
| Final gravity: | 1007 | Mash temperature: | 65ºC |
| Alcohol content: | 3.20% | Mash time: | 90 minutes |
| Bittering units: | 23 | Boil time: | 90 minutes |
| Final volume: | 23 litres | | |

In the tun

| | |
|---|---|
| Pale malt | 2890g |
| Crystal malt | 45g |
| Wheat flour | 210g |

In the boiler

| | |
|---|---|
| Challenger hops (6.2%) | 46g (start of boil) |
| Maltose syrup | 338g (after 45 minutes) |
| Challenger hops | 9g (last 15 minutes) |
| Irish Moss | 5g (last 15 minutes) |

Malt extract version
Partial mash required. Replace the pale malt with 2100g of diastatic malt extract.

# DAN YR AWEL SPECIAL

*A very smooth, refreshing ale, with a good hop character.*

| | | | |
|---|---|---|---|
| Original gravity: | 1040 | Mash liquor: | 11 litres |
| Final gravity: | 1007 | Mash temperature: | 65⁰C |
| Alcohol content: | 4.20% | Mash time: | 90 minutes |
| Bittering units: | 35 | Boil time: | 90 minutes |
| Final volume: | 23 litres | | |

In the tun

| | |
|---|---|
| Pale malt | 4480g |
| Chocolate malt | 25g |

In the boiler

| | |
|---|---|
| Northdown hops (7.5%) | 58g (start of boil) |
| Styrian Golding hops | 12 g (last 15 minutes) |
| Irish Moss | 5g (last 15 minutes) |

Malt extract version
No mash required. Replace the pale malt with 3250g of light-coloured malt extract.

# DRUID'S ALE

*A pale-coloured ale, with a stunning aroma from the use of 'noble' hops. With a good malt flavour to counter the bitterness.*

| | | | |
|---|---|---|---|
| Original gravity: | 1047 | Mash liquor: | 13 litres |
| Final gravity: | 1008 | Mash temperature: | 66ºC |
| Alcohol content: | 5.00% | Mash time: | 2 hours |
| Bittering units: | 35 | Boil time: | 2 hours |
| Final volume: | 23 litres | | |

In the tun

| | |
|---|---|
| Pale malt | 5150g |
| Crystal malt | 55g |
| Chocolate malt | 105g |

In the boiler

| | |
|---|---|
| Northern Brewer hops (5.7%) | 54g (start of boil) |
| Halletauer hops (1.5%) | 88g (start of boil) |
| Tettnang hops | 28g (last 15 minutes) |
| Irish Moss | 5g (last 15 minutes) |
| Tettnang hops | 10g (dry hops in cask) |

Notes:
Copper hops were calculated assuming a mix of 70% Northern Brewer and 30% Halletauer. If you are unable to purchase Tettnang hops then you may substitute the exact quantity with Saaz.

Malt extract version
No mash required. Replace the pale malt with 3750g of light-coloured malt extract.

## DUNRAVEN STRONG BITTER

*A pale, well balanced country bitter.*

| | | | |
|---|---|---|---|
| Original gravity: | 1037 | Mash liquor: | 9 litres |
| Final gravity: | 1007 | Mash temperature: | 65°C |
| Alcohol content | 3.90% | Mash time: | 90 minutes |
| Bittering units: | 29 | Boil time: | 90 minutes |
| Final volume: | 23 litres | | |

### In the tun

| | |
|---|---|
| Pale malt | 2615g |
| Crystal malt | 300g |
| Torrified wheat | 605g |

### In the boiler

| | |
|---|---|
| Target hops (8.7%) | 42g (start of boil) |
| Invert sugar | 502g (after 45 minutes) |
| Target hops | 8g (last 15 minutes) |
| Irish Moss | 5g (last 15 minutes) |
| Target hops | 5g (dry hops in cask) |

Malt extract version
Partial mash required. Replace the pale malt with 1900g of diastatic malt extract.

# GEMMA'S GOLDEN ALE

*A beautifully balanced pale golden beer, with a huge hop character.*

| | | | |
|---|---|---|---|
| Original gravity: | 1048 | Mash liquor: | 14 litres |
| Final gravity: | 1010 | Mash temperature: | 65°C |
| Alcohol content: | 4.90% | Mash time: | 90 minutes |
| Bittering units: | 50 | Boil time: | 2 hours |
| Final volume: | 23 litres | | |

In the tun
Pale malt                    5405 g (start of boil)

127

In the boiler
Progress hops (5.5%)      114 g (start of boil)
Progress hops                20g (last 15 minutes)
Irish Moss                    5g (last 15 minutes)

Malt extract version
No mash required. Replace the pale malt with 3950g of light-coloured malt extract.

# GLAMORGAN BITTER

*A beer with great hop aroma and flavour.*

| | | | |
|---|---|---|---|
| Original gravity: | 1034 | Mash liquor: | 10 litres |
| Final gravity: | 1008 | Mash temperature: | 65°C |
| Alcohol content: | 3.40% | Mash time: | 90 minutes |
| Bittering units: | 32 | Boil time: | 90 minutes |
| Final volume: | 23 litres | | |

In the tun

| | |
|---|---|
| Pale malt | 3760g |
| Chocolate malt | 80g |

In the boiler

| | |
|---|---|
| Progress hops (5.5%) | 73g (start of boil) |
| Styrian Golding hops | 15g (last 15 minutes) |
| Irish Moss | 5g (last 15 minutes) |
| Styrian Golding | 5g (dry hops in cask) |

Malt extract version

No mash required. Replace the pale malt with 2750g of light-coloured malt extract.

# GLAMORGAN'S GLORY

*This ale, with its full body and lingering bitterness, must surely be one of the finest premium ales in the book. A premium type bitter, with ample malt and hop character to keep your tastebuds working.*

| | | | |
|---|---|---|---|
| Original gravity: | 1045 | Mash liquor: | 13 litres |
| Final gravity: | 1009 | Mash temperature: | 65°C |
| Alcohol content: | 4.70% | Mash time: | 2 hours |
| Bittering units: | 41 | Boil time: | 2 hours |
| Final volume: | 23 litres | | |

In the tun

| | |
|---|---|
| Pale malt | 3700g |
| Crystal malt | 330g |
| Wheat malt | 125g |
| Amber malt | 250g |
| Torrified wheat | 330g |

In the boiler

| | |
|---|---|
| Target hops (8.7%) | 29g (start of boil) |
| Omega hops (8.5%) | 30g (start of boil) |
| Maltose syrup | 302g (after 1 hour) |
| Goldings hops | 12g (last 15 minutes) |
| Irish Moss | 5g (last 15 minutes) |
| Goldings hops | 5g (dry hops in cask) |

Notes:
Substitute Omega with 29g of Challenger (6.2%) if unavailable.

Malt extract version
Partial mash required. Replace the pale malt with 2700g of diastatic malt extract.

# INGLENOOK

*A very malty and potent winter-style ale. One to be enjoyed by the fireside.*

| | | | |
|---|---|---|---|
| Original gravity: | 1072 | Mash liquor: | 18 litres |
| Final gravity: | 1025 | Mash temperature: | 67ºC |
| Alcohol content: | 6.00% | Mash time: | 2 hours |
| Bittering units: | 28 | Boil time: | 2 hours |
| Final volume: | 23 litres | | |

In the tun

| | |
|---|---|
| Pale malt | 6907g |
| Crystal malt | 700g |
| Torrified wheat | 620g |

In the boiler

| | |
|---|---|
| Challenger hops (6.2%) | 56g (start of boil) |
| Goldings hops | 10g (last 15 minutes) |
| Irish Moss | 5g (last 15 minutes) |

Malt extract version

Partial mash required. Replace the pale malt with 5045g of diastatic malt extract.

# IONIAN ALE

*A superb ale, which has a full body and a mouth-filling presence of malt and hops.*

| | | | |
|---|---|---|---|
| Original gravity: | 1043 | Mash liquor: | 12 litres |
| Final gravity: | 1010 | Mash temperature: | 66⁰C |
| Alcohol content: | 4.30% | Mash time: | 90 minutes |
| Bittering units: | 33 | Boil time | 90 minutes |
| Final volume: | 23 litres | | |

In the tun

| | |
|---|---|
| Pale malt | 3970g |
| Crystal malt | 320 g |
| Wheat malt | 295g |
| Amber malt | 320g |

In the boiler

| | |
|---|---|
| Challenger hops (6.2%) | 67g (start of boil) |
| Fuggles hops | 13g (last 15 minutes) |
| Irish Moss | 5g (last 15 minutes) |

Malt extract version

Partial mash required. Replace the pale malt with 2900g of diastatic malt extract.

## JOHN'S PREMIUM PALE ALE

*A full-bodied ale, with a fine aroma and bitterness level.*

| | | | |
|---|---|---|---|
| Original gravity: | 1047 | Mash liquor: | 13 litres |
| Final gravity: | 1010 | Mash temperature: | 66°C |
| Alcohol content: | 4.80% | Mash time: | 2 hours |
| Bittering units: | 42 | Boil time: | 2 hours |
| Final volume: | 23 litres | | |

In the tun

| | |
|---|---|
| Pale malt | 5100g |
| Crystal malt | 215g |

In the boiler

| | |
|---|---|
| Goldings hops (4.0%) | 131g (start of boil) |
| Goldings hops | 26g (last 15 minutes) |
| Irish Moss | 5g (last 15 minutes) |
| Goldings hops | 5 g (dry hops in cask) |

Malt extract version
No mash required. Replace the pale malt with 3700g of light-coloured malt extract.

# KAREN'S BITTER

*A pale-coloured bitter with a strong hop aroma.*

| | | | |
|---|---|---|---|
| Original gravity: | 1039 | Mash liquor: | 10 litres |
| Final gravity: | 1009 | Mash temperature: | 650C |
| Alcohol content: | 3.90% | Mash time: | 90 minutes |
| Bittering units: | 33 | Boil time: | 90 minutes |
| Final volume: | 23 litres | | |

In the tun

| | |
|---|---|
| Pale malt | 2770g |
| Crystal malt | 140g |
| Torrified wheat | 180g |

In the boiler

| | |
|---|---|
| Challenger hops (6.2%) | 67g (start of boil) |
| Invert sugar | 923g (after 45 minutes) |
| Challenger hops | 13g (last 15 minutes) |
| Irish Moss | 5g (last 15 minutes) |
| Challenger | 8g (dry hops in cask) |

Malt extract version
Partial mash required. Replace the pale malt with 2000g of diastatic malt extract.

133

# LAST CHANCE BITTER

*An easy drinking gold/amber colour bitter ale with a malty edge.*

| | | | |
|---|---|---|---|
| Original gravity: | 1038 | Mash liquor: | 11 litres |
| Final gravity: | 1009 | Mash temperature: | 65°C |
| Alcohol content: | 3.70% | Mash time: | 90 minutes |
| Bittering units: | 30 | Boil time: | 2 hours |
| Final volume: | 23 litres | | |

In the tun

| | |
|---|---|
| Pale malt | 3730g |
| Crystal malt | 610g |

In the boiler

| | |
|---|---|
| Fuggles hops (3.3%) | 80g (start of boil) |
| Goldings hops (4.0%) | 28g (start of boil) |
| Goldings hops | 22g (last 15 minutes) |
| Irish Moss | 5g (last 15 minutes) |

Malt extract version
No mash required. Replace the pale malt with 2700g of light-coloured malt extract.

# MAHOGANY

*A mouth-filling combination of malt and hops, with an excellent aroma.*

| | | | |
|---|---|---|---|
| Original gravity: | 1044 | Mash liquor: | 12 litres |
| Final gravity: | 1009 | Mash temperature: | 66ºC |
| Alcohol content: | 4.50% | Mash time: | 90 minutes |
| Bittering units: | 30 | Boil time: | 90 minutes |
| Final volume: | 23 litres | | |

In the tun

| | |
|---|---|
| Pale malt | 3220g |
| Crystal malt | 360g |
| Torrified wheat | 595g |

In the boiler

| | |
|---|---|
| Target hops (8.7%) | 39g (start of boil) |
| Styrian Golding hops (3.7%) | 10 g (start of boil) |
| Invert sugar | 596g (after 45 minutes) |
| Styrian Golding hops | 10 g (last 15 minutes) |
| Irish Moss | 5g (last 15 minutes) |

Malt extract version
Partial mash required. Replace the pale malt with 2350g of diastatic malt extract.

## MARC'S PALE ALE

*A very drinkable and tasty session bitter*

| | | | |
|---|---|---|---|
| Original gravity: | 1035 | Mash liquor: | 10 litres |
| Final gravity: | 1007 | Mash temperature: | 65ºC |
| Alcohol content: | 3.60% | Mash time: | 90 minutes |
| Bittering units: | 27 | Boil time: | 2 hours |
| Final volume: | 23 litres | | |

In the tun
| | |
|---|---|
| Pale malt | 3560g |
| Crystal malt | 195g |
| Wheat flour | 195g |

In the boiler
| | |
|---|---|
| Goldings hops (4.0%) | 84g (start of boil) |
| Fuggles hops | 16g (last 15 minutes) |
| Irish Moss | 5g (last 15 minutes) |

Malt extract version
Partial mash required. Replace the pale malt with 2600g of diastatic malt extract.

# MARKET BEST BITTER

*A thirst quenching ale, with a superb hop aroma from the unusual use solely of Styrian hops.*

| | | | |
|---|---|---|---|
| Original gravity: | 1040 | Mash liquor: | 11 litres |
| Final gravity: | 1009 | Mash temperature: | 650C |
| Alcohol content: | 4.00% | Mash time: | 90 minutes |
| Bittering units: | 38 | Boil time: | 2 hours |
| Final volume: | 23 litres | | |

In the tun

| | |
|---|---|
| Pale malt | 4295g |
| Crystal malt | 225g |

In the boiler

| | |
|---|---|
| Styrian Golding hops (3.7%) | 128g (start of boil) |
| Styrian Golding hops | 26g (last 15 minutes) |
| Irish Moss | 5g (last 15 minutes) |

Malt extract version

No mash required. Replace the pale malt with 3150g of light-coloured malt extract.

## NO REGRETS

*A full-flavoured ale which you won't regret brewing, except that you might wish you'd made twice as much.*

| | | | |
|---|---|---|---|
| Original gravity: | 1048 | Mash liquor: | 14 litres |
| Final gravity: | 1011 | Mash temperature: | 65ºC |
| Alcohol content: | 4.8% | Mash time: | 2 hours |
| Bittering units: | 40 | Boil time: | 2 hours |
| Final volume: | 23 litres | | |

In the tun

| | |
|---|---|
| Pale malt | 4905g |
| Crystal malt | 545g |

In the boiler

| | |
|---|---|
| Challenger hops (6.2%) | 40g (start of boil) |
| Target hops (8.7%) | 29g (last 15 minutes) |
| Northdown hops | 14g (last 15 minutes) |
| Irish Moss | 5g (last 15 minutes) |

Malt extract version

No mash required. Replace the pale malt with 3600g of light-coloured malt extract

# OLD LINGUIST

*Strong, pale coloured ale. This will quickly take control of your tongue.*

| | | | |
|---|---|---|---|
| Original gravity: | 1060 | Mash liquor: | 17 litres |
| Final gravity: | 1015 | Mash temperature: | 66ºC |
| Alcohol content: | 5.80% | Mash time: | 2 hours |
| Bittering units: | 30 | Boil time: | 2 hours |
| Final volume: | 23 litres | | |

In the tun
Pale malt                6760g

In the boiler
Fuggles hops (3.3%)      80g (start of boil)
Goldings hops (4.0%)     28g (start of boil)
Goldings hops            22g (last 15 minutes)
Irish Moss               5g (last 15 minutes)

Malt extract version
No mash required. Replace the pale malt with 4950g of light-coloured malt extract.

## OLD RAMBLER

*A potent malty-tasting ale. You'll certainly be rambling after a few of these.*

| | | | |
|---|---|---|---|
| Original gravity: | 1070 | Mash liquor: | 20 litres |
| Final gravity: | 1014 | Mash temperature: | 67°C |
| Alcohol content: | 7.20% | Mash time: | 2 hours |
| Bittering units: | 35 | Boil time: | 2 hours |
| Final volume: | 23 litres | | |

In the tun

| | |
|---|---|
| Pale malt | 7740g |
| Black malt | 150g |

In the boiler

| | |
|---|---|
| Goldings hops (4.0%) | 109 g (start of boil) |
| Goldings hops | 22g (last 15 minutes) |
| Irish Moss | 5g (last 15 minutes) |

Malt extract version

No mash required. Replace the pale malt with 5650g of light-coloured malt extract.

# OLD RUBY ALE

*A full-bodied ale, with a rich full malt feel in the mouth.*

| | | | |
|---|---|---|---|
| Original gravity: | 1050 | Mash liquor: | 13 litres |
| Final gravity: | 1012 | Mash temperature: | 65°C |
| Alcohol content: | 4.9% | Mash time: | 2 hours |
| Bittering units: | 28 | Boil time: | 2 hours |
| Final volume: | 23 litres | | |

In the tun

| | |
|---|---|
| Pale malt | 3585g |
| Crystal malt | 210g |
| Chocolate malt | 105g |
| Torrified wheat | 210g |

In the boiler

| | |
|---|---|
| Challenger hops (6.2%) | 56g (start of boil) |
| Invert sugar | 1092g (after 1 hour) |
| Challenger hops | 11g (last 15 minutes) |
| Irish Moss | 5g (last 15 minutes) |

Malt extract version
Partial mash required. Replace the pale malt with 2600g of diastatic malt extract.

# PEN y BONT BITTER

*Lovely refreshing pale ale with plenty of hop flavours. Very popular with many home brewers.*

| | | | |
|---|---|---|---|
| Original gravity: | 1036 | Mash liquor: | 10 litres |
| Final gravity: | 1008 | Mash temperature: | 65ºC |
| Alcohol content: | 3.60% | Mash time: | 90 minutes |
| Bittering units: | 40 | Boil time: | 2 hours |
| Final volume: | 23 litres | | |

In the tun

| | |
|---|---|
| Pale malt | 3980g |
| Crystal malt | 80g |

142

In the boiler

| | |
|---|---|
| Challenger hops (6.2%) | 81g (start of boil) |
| Challenger hops | 16g (last 15 minutes) |
| Irish Moss | 5g (last 15 minutes) |

Malt extract version
No mash required. Replace the pale malt with 2900g of light-coloured malt extract.

# PITHEAD BITTER

*A full-flavoured brew.*

| | | | |
|---|---|---|---|
| Original gravity: | 1044 | Mash liquor: | 12 litres |
| Final gravity: | 1009 | Mash temperature: | 65°C |
| Alcohol content: | 4.50% | Mash time: | 90 minutes |
| Bittering units: | 32 | Boil time: | 2 hours |
| Final volume: | 23 litres | | |

In the tun

| | |
|---|---|
| Pale malt | 4640g |
| Crystal malt | 350g |

In the boiler

| | |
|---|---|
| Fuggles hops (3.3%) | 85g (start of boil) |
| Goldings hops (4.0%) | 30g (start of boil) |
| Goldings hops | 24g (last 15 minutes) |
| Irish Moss | 5g (last 15 minutes) |

Malt extract version
No mash required. Replace the pale malt with 3400g of light-coloured malt extract.

143

# PITSHAFT ALE

*A bitter beer with great malt character and a lovely aroma… why not sink a few?*

| | | | |
|---|---|---|---|
| Original gravity: | 1038 | Mash liquor: | 11 litres |
| Final gravity: | 1009 | Mash temperature: | 650C |
| Alcohol content: | 3.80% | Mash time: | 90 minutes |
| Bittering units: | 30 | Boil time: | 90 minutes |
| Final volume: | 23 litres | | |

### In the tun

| | |
|---|---|
| Pale malt | 4080g |
| Crystal malt | 195g |
| Chocolate malt | 20g |

### In the boiler

| | |
|---|---|
| Challenger hops (6.2%) | 60g (start of boil) |
| Challenger hops | 12g (last 15 minutes) |
| Irish Moss | 5g (last 15 minutes) |

### Malt extract version
No mash required. Replace the pale malt with 3000g of light-coloured malt extract.

# PLOUGHMAN'S BEST BITTER

*Good balance of malt and hops, quite a hoppy finish. Great aroma from the Progress hops. The malt is smooth in the mouth, balanced well by a good level of bitterness. Ideal for drinking with a ploughman's or any other sort of lunch*

| | | | |
|---|---|---|---|
| Original gravity: | 1038 | Mash liquor: | 11 litres |
| Final gravity: | 1009 | Mash temperature: | 65°C |
| Alcohol content: | 3.80% | Mash time: | 90 minutes |
| Bittering units: | 35 | Boil time: | 90 minutes |
| Final volume: | 23 litres | | |

In the tun

| | |
|---|---|
| Pale malt | 3965g |
| Crystal malt | 345g |

In the boiler

| | |
|---|---|
| Challenger hops (6.2%) | 71g (start of boil) |
| Progress hops | 14g (last 15 minutes) |
| Irish Moss | 5g (last 15 minutes) |
| Progress | 7 g (dry hops in cask) |

Malt extract version
No mash required. Replace the pale malt with 2900g of light-coloured malt extract.

# POLITICAL ALE

*Elect to brew this bitter, and you'll be MPressed by its smooth, thirst-quenching taste and honest character.*

| | | | |
|---|---|---|---|
| Original gravity: | 1032 | Mash liquor: | 9 litres |
| Final gravity: | 1007 | Mash temperature: | 66°C |
| Alcohol content: | 3.20% | Mash time: | 90 minutes |
| Bittering units: | 28 | Boil time: | 2 hours |
| Final volume: | 23 litres | | |

In the tun

| | |
|---|---|
| Pale malt | 2565g |
| Crystal malt | 105g |
| Torrified wheat | 275g |

In the boiler

| | |
|---|---|
| WGV hops (4.5%) | 15g (start of boil) |
| Challenger hops (6.2%) | 34g (start of boil) |
| Bramling Cross hops (5.5%) | 13g (start of boil) |
| Invert sugar | 479g (after 1 hour) |
| WGV hops | 12g (last 15 minutes) |
| Irish Moss | 5g (last 15 minutes) |

Malt extract version

Partial mash required. Replace the pale malt with 1900g of diastatic malt extract.

# PREMIUM PALE

*A premium, fine tasting, pale-coloured ale, extremely popular when sampled in the shop*

| | | | |
|---|---|---|---|
| Original gravity: | 1040 | Mash liquor: | 11 litres |
| Final gravity: | 1009 | Mash temperature: | 65ºC |
| Alcohol content: | 4.00% | Mash time: | 90 minutes |
| Bittering units: | 40 | Boil time: | 2 hours |
| Final volume: | 23 litres | | |

In the tun

Pale malt                 4500g

In the boiler

Styrian Golding hops (3.7%)   135g (start of boil)
Styrian Golding hops          27g (last 15 minutes)
Irish Moss                    5g (last 15 minutes)

Malt extract version
No mash required. Replace the pale malt with 3300g of light-coloured malt extract.

# REFERENDUM ALE

*A full-bodied ale, with some hop notes. Try it, and decide for yourself!*

| | | | |
|---|---|---|---|
| Original gravity: | 1048 | Mash liquor: | 13 litres |
| Final gravity: | 1008 | Mash temperature: | 65°C |
| Alcohol content: | 5.20% | Mash time: | 90 minutes |
| Bittering units: | 28 | Boil time: | 2 hours |
| Final volume: | 23 litres | | |

In the tun

| | |
|---|---|
| Pale malt | 4555g |
| Crystal malt | 495g |
| Torrified wheat | 440g |

In the boiler

| | |
|---|---|
| Challenger hops (6.2%) | 56g (start of boil) |
| Goldings hops | 10g (last 15 minutes) |
| Irish Moss | 5g (last 15 minutes) |

Malt extract version
Partial mash required. Replace the pale malt with 3300g of diastatic malt extract.

# RIVERSIDE BITTER

*A beer with a full malt flavour, with just the right amount of bitterness, and a low alcohol content – just right for a session bitter.*

| | | | |
|---|---|---|---|
| Original gravity: | 1034 | Mash liquor: | 10 litres |
| Final gravity: | 1008 | Mash temperature: | 65ºC |
| Alcohol content: | 3.40% | Mash time: | 90 minutes |
| Bittering units | : 24 | Boil time: | 90 minutes |
| Final volume | : 23 litres | | |

In the tun

| | |
|---|---|
| Pale malt | 3405g |
| Crystal malt | 465g |

In the boiler

| | |
|---|---|
| Challenger hops (6.2%) | 48g (start of boil) |
| Fuggles hops | 10g (last 15 minutes) |
| Irish Moss | 5g (last 15 minutes) |

Malt extract version
No mash required. Replace the pale malt with 2500g of light-coloured malt extract.

# SCOTTISH HEAVY

*A rich tasting example of a classic style*

| | | | |
|---|---|---|---|
| Original gravity: | 1050 | Mash liquor: | 14 litres |
| Final gravity: | 1011 | Mash temperature: | 66°C |
| Alcohol content: | 5.00% | Mash time: | 90 minutes |
| Bittering units: | 34 | Boil time: | 2 hours |
| Final volume: | 23 litres | | |

In the tun

| | |
|---|---|
| Pale malt | 5575g |
| Black malt | 55g |

In the boiler

| | |
|---|---|
| Goldings hops (4.0%) | 106g (start of boil) |
| Goldings hops | 21g (last 15 minutes) |
| Irish Moss | 5g (last 15 minutes) |

Malt extract version
No mash required. Replace the pale malt with 4100g of light-coloured malt extract.

# STRONG DRAUGHT ALE

*A well-balanced strong ale. Drink with caution.*

| | | | |
|---|---|---|---|
| Original gravity: | 1052 | Mash liquor: | 15 litres |
| Final gravity: | 1012 | Mash temperature: | 65°C |
| Alcohol content: | 5.20% | Mash time: | 2 hours |
| Bittering units: | 28 | Boil time: | 2 hours |
| Final volume: | 23 litres | | |

In the tun

| | |
|---|---|
| Pale malt | 5695g |
| Chocolate malt | 175g |

In the boiler

| | |
|---|---|
| Progress hops (5.5%) | 64g (start of boil) |
| Styrian Golding hops | 13g (last 15 minutes) |
| Irish Moss | 5g (last 15 minutes) |
| Styrian Golding hops | 5g (dry hops in cask) |

Malt extract version

No mash required. Replace the pale malt with 4150g of light-coloured malt extract.

# STYRIAN STUNNER

*A very pale beer, with exceptional hop flavour and character provided by the Styrian hops.*

| | | | |
|---|---|---|---|
| Original gravity: | 1040 | Mash liquor: | 11 litres |
| Final gravity: | 1009 | Mash temperature: | 65°C |
| Alcohol content: | 4.10% | Mash time: | 90 minutes |
| Bittering units: | 21 | Boil time: | 2 hours |
| Final volume: | 23 litres | | |

In the tun
Pale malt                           4560g

In the boiler
Styrian Golding hops (3.7%)  71g (start of boil)
Styrian Golding hops         14g (last 15 minutes)
Irish Moss                   5g (last 15 minutes)

Malt extract version
No mash required. Replace the pale malt with 3350g of light-coloured malt extract.

# THORSHEAD

*This beer has a rich malty character, with a hoppy finish. Drink too many and you'll have a thor head too!*

| | | | |
|---|---|---|---|
| Original gravity: | 1059 | Mash liquor: | 17 litres |
| Final gravity: | 1012 | Mash temperature: | 66°C |
| Alcohol content: | 6.00% | Mash time: | 2 hours |
| Bittering units: | 35 | Boil time: | 2 hours |
| Final volume: | 23 litres | | |

In the tun

| | |
|---|---|
| Pale malt | 6520g |
| Chocolate malt | 135g |

153

In the boiler

| | |
|---|---|
| Progress hops (5.5%) | 80g (start of boil) |
| Styrian Golding hops | 16g (last 15 minutes) |
| Irish Moss | 5g (last 15 minutes) |

Malt extract version
No mash required. Replace the pale malt with 4750g of light-coloured malt extract.

# TOP NOTCH BITTER

*A beer with a full maltiness in the mouth, a sweetish brew with a pleasing hop presence.*

| | | | |
|---|---|---|---|
| Original gravity: | 1050 | Mash liquor: | 13 litres |
| Final gravity: | 1012 | Mash temperature: | 65°C |
| Alcohol content: | 4.9% | Mash time: | 2 hours |
| Bittering units: | 28 | Boil time: | 2 hours |
| Final volume: | 23 litres | | |

In the tun

| | |
|---|---|
| Pale malt | 3550g |
| Crystal malt | 205g |
| Torrified wheat | 205g |

In the boiler

| | |
|---|---|
| Challenger hops (6.2%) | 56g (start of boil) |
| Invert sugar | 1183g (after 1 hour) |
| Challenger hops | 11g (last 15 minutes) |
| Irish Moss | 5g (last 15 minutes) |

Malt extract version
Partial mash required. Replace the pale malt with 2600g of diastatic malt extract.

# TOWER PIT

*A strong, pale-coloured ale, with a lasting deep flavour*

| | | | |
|---|---|---|---|
| Original gravity: | 1048 | Mash liquor: | 14 litres |
| Final gravity: | 1009 | Mash temperature: | 65ºC |
| Alcohol content: | 5.00% | Mash time: | 90 minutes |
| Bittering units: | 30 | Boil time: | 90 minutes |
| Final volume: | 23 litres | | |

In the tun
| | |
|---|---|
| Pale malt | 5230g |
| Crystal malt | 190g |

In the boiler
| | |
|---|---|
| Challenger (6.2%) | 60g (start of boil) |
| Challenger hops | 12g (last 15 minutes) |
| Irish Moss | 5g (last 15 minutes) |

Malt extract version
No mash required. Replace the pale malt with 3800g of light-coloured malt extract.

# VALHALLA

*A malty brew with plenty of flavour from the coloured malts, and with a well balanced-bitterness. Fit for the gods!*

| | | | |
|---|---|---|---|
| Original gravity: | 1052 | Mash liquor: | 13 litres |
| Final gravity: | 1012 | Mash temperature: | 66°C |
| Alcohol content: | 5.2% | Mash time: | 2 hours |
| Bittering units: | 38 | Boil time: | 2 hours |
| Final volume: | 23 litres | | |

In the tun

| | |
|---|---|
| Pale malt | 4750g |
| Crystal malt | 355g |
| Wheat malt | 355g |
| Amber malt | 355g |
| Roast barley | 120g |

In the boiler

| | |
|---|---|
| Challenger hops (6.2%) | 77g (start of boil) |
| Fuggles hops | 15g (last 15 minutes) |
| Irish Moss | 5g (last 15 minutes) |

Malt extract version
Partial mash required. Replace the pale malt with 3450g of diastatic malt extract.

# WYNDHAM WINDER

*A dark chestnut-coloured ale, with a full mouth-filling flavour from the malt and hops. The use of Goldings provides a brilliant aroma.*

| | | | |
|---|---|---|---|
| Original gravity: | 1045 | Mash liquor: | 13 litres |
| Final gravity: | 1010 | Mash temperature: | 65°C |
| Alcohol content: | 4.50% | Mash time: | 90 minutes |
| Bittering units: | 32 | Boil time: | 2 hours |
| Final volume: | 23 litres | | |

In the tun

| | |
|---|---|
| Pale malt | 4320g |
| Crystal malt | 825g |

In the boiler

| | |
|---|---|
| Fuggles hops(3.3%) | 48g (start of boil) |
| Goldings hops (4.0%) | 60g (start of boil) |
| Goldings hops | 22g (last 15 minutes) |
| Irish Moss | 5g (last 15 minutes) |
| Goldings hops | 5g (dry hops in cask) |

Malt extract version

No mash required. Replace the pale malt with 3150g of light-coloured malt extract.

# Mild and dark ales

## COUNTRYWIDE MILD

*An easy-drinking dark mild. Although an undemanding beer, it is very pleasant to drink.*

| | | | |
|---|---|---|---|
| Original gravity: | 1032 | Mash liquor: | 9 litres |
| Final gravity: | 1008 | Mash temperature: | 64ºC |
| Alcohol content: | 3.10% | Mash time: | 90 minutes |
| Bittering units: | 22 | Boil time: | 90 minutes |
| Final volume: | 23 litres | | |

In the tun
| | |
|---|---|
| Pale malt | 3150g |
| Black malt | 140g |

In the boiler
| | |
|---|---|
| Challenger hops (6.2%) | 44g (start of boil) |
| Maltose syrup | 247g (after 45 minutes) |
| Goldings hops | 9g (last 15 minutes) |
| Irish Moss | 5g (last 15 minutes) |

Malt extract version
No mash required. Replace the pale malt with 2300g of light-coloured malt extract.

# HODDESDON DARK

*An easy drinking, smooth malty dark mild with a pleasant roast barley flavour coming through.*

| | | | |
|---|---|---|---|
| Original gravity: | 1037 | Mash liquor: | 11 litres |
| Final gravity: | 1008 | Mash temperature: | 63ºC |
| Alcohol content: | 3.70% | Mash time: | 90 minutes |
| Bittering units: | 26 | Boil time: | 90 minutes |
| Final volume: | 23 litres | | |

In the tun

| | |
|---|---|
| Pale malt | 3390g |
| Crystal malt | 340g |
| Roast barley | 170g |
| Torrified wheat | 340g |

In the boiler

| | |
|---|---|
| Challenger hops (6.2%) | 52g (start of boil) |
| Goldings hops | 10g (last 15 minutes) |
| Irish Moss | 5g (last 15 minutes) |

Malt extract version
Partial mash required. Replace the pale malt with 2500g of diastatic malt extract.

# Porters and stouts

## BLACK DIAMOND

*Tasty and richly flavoured porter style beer.*

| | | | |
|---|---|---|---|
| Original gravity: | 1049 | Mash liquor: | 14 litres |
| Final gravity: | 1009 | Mash temperature: | 66ºC |
| Alcohol content: | 5.20% | Mash time: | 2 hours |
| Bittering units: | 33 | Boil time: | 2 hours |
| Final volume: | 23 litres | | |

In the tun

| | |
|---|---|
| Pale malt | 3575g |
| Crystal malt | 660g |
| Chocolate malt | 385g |
| Torrified wheat | 440g |

In the boiler

| | |
|---|---|
| Target hops (8.7%) | 47g (start of boil) |
| Maltose syrup | 440g (after 1 hour) |
| Goldings hops | 9g (last 15 minutes) |
| Irish Moss | 5g (last 15 minutes) |

Malt extract version
Partial mash required. Replace the pale malt with 2600g of diastatic malt extract.

# BLACKNESS

*A black beer with superb character, derived from the use of dark malts and a high rate of hops*

| | | | |
|---|---|---|---|
| Original gravity: | 1055 | Mash liquor: | 16 litres |
| Final gravity: | 1012 | Mash temperature: | 66°C |
| Alcohol content: | 5.50% | Mash time: | 2 hours |
| Bittering units: | 40 | Boil time: | 2 hours |
| Final volume: | 23 litres | | |

In the tun

| | |
|---|---|
| Pale malt | 5645g |
| Crystal malt | 410g |
| Black malt | 205g |

In the boiler

| | |
|---|---|
| Fuggles hops (3.3%) | 45g (start of boil) |
| Goldings hops (4.0%) | 88g (start of boil) |
| Goldings hops | 22g (last 15 minutes) |
| Irish Moss | 5g (last 15 minutes) |
| Goldings hops | 10 g (dry hops in cask) |

Malt extract version
No mash required. Replace the pale malt with 4100g of light-coloured malt extract.

eal Ales for the Home Brewer

# COAL FACE DARK

*A strong dark stout tasting like ale.*

| | | | |
|---|---|---|---|
| Original gravity: | 1059 | Mash liquor: | 17 litres |
| Final gravity: | 1012 | Mash temperature: | 66°C |
| Alcohol content: | 6.00% | Mash time: | 2 hours |
| Bittering units: | 27 | Boil time: | 2 hours |
| Final volume: | 23 litres | | |

In the tun

| | |
|---|---|
| Pale malt | 6090g |
| Crystal malt | 300g |
| Roast barley | 300g |

In the boiler

| | |
|---|---|
| Challenger hops (6.2%) | 54g (start of boil) |
| Challenger hops | 11g (last 15 minutes) |
| Irish Moss | 5g (last 15 minutes) |

Malt extract version
No mash required. Replace the pale malt with 4450g of light-coloured malt extract.

# COAL SEAM

*A strong, very dark stout-type beer, with a superb balance of malt and hops.*

| | | | |
|---|---|---|---|
| Original gravity: | 1060 | Mash liquor: | 17 litres |
| Final gravity: | 1013 | Mash temperature: | 66ºC |
| Alcohol content: | 6.00% | Mash time: | 2 hours |
| Bittering units: | 42 | Boil time: | 2 hours |
| Final volume: | 23 litres | | |

In the tun

| | |
|---|---|
| Pale malt | 4610g |
| Crystal malt | 2025g |
| Black malt | 140g |
| Roast barley | 210g |

In the boiler

| | | |
|---|---|---|
| Challenger hops (6.2%) | 85g (start of boil) | 55g (7.1) |
| Fuggles hops | 17g (last 15 minutes) | 25g (5%) |
| Irish Moss | 5g (last 15 minutes) | |

Malt extract version
No mash required. Replace the pale malt with 3350g of light-coloured malt extract.

163

# MARKET PORTER

*A very tasty ale, with complex flavours from the dark malts.*

| | | | |
|---|---|---|---|
| Original gravity: | 1036 | Mash liquor: | 10 litres |
| Final gravity: | 1007 | Mash temperature: | 66°C |
| Alcohol content: | 3.70% | Mash time: | 90 minutes |
| Bittering units: | 25 | Boil time: | 2 hours |
| Final volume: | 23 litres | | |

In the tun

| | |
|---|---|
| Pale malt | 3420g |
| Chocolate malt | 120g |
| Crystal malt | 325g |
| Roast Barley | 120g |

In the boiler

| | |
|---|---|
| Northdown hops (7.5%) | 42g (start of boil) |
| Invert sugar | 80 g (after 1 hour) |
| Northdown hops | 8g (last 15 minutes) |
| Irish Moss | 5g (last 15 minutes) |

Notes:
Invert sugar added to arrive at Original Gravity.

Malt extract version
No mash required. Replace the pale malt with 2500g of light-coloured malt extract.

# Useful addresses

If your local home brew shop doesn't stock a particular product and hasn't got an alternative, then you can contact the following, who should be able to point you in the right direction.

BRUPAKS
2 Kennedy Avenue
Fixby
Huddersfield
HD2 2HJ
Telephone 01484 841116
www.brupacks.com

YOUNGS HOMEBREW LTD
Unit A
Cross Street
Bradley
Bilston
WV14 8DL
Telephone 01902 353053
www.youngshomebrew.co.uk

OTHER USEFUL ADDRESSES
Tuckers Maltings
Teign Road
Newton Abbot
TQ12 4AA
Telephone (01626) 334002
www.edwintucker.com

OTHER USEFUL ADDRESSES

**Craft Brewers Association**
82 Elmfield Rd
London
SW17 8AN
www.craftbrewing.org.uk

INTERNET LINKS
**Jims Homebrew Forum** -
www.jimsbeerkit.co.uk
A stunning wealth of information and with extremely helpful and knowledgeable members this site is a must have for your bookmarks.

**American Homebrewers Association** -
www.homebrewersassociation.org

# About the author

*R*eal Ales for the Home Brewer was written by Marc Ollosson between 1992 and 1996 and first published in 1997 by Nexus Special Interest.

The book was instantly successful with brewers, both beginner and seasoned alike, and contained over 100 quality recipes. Each one tried and tested many times by the author and/or customers of the homebrew shop Marc owned.

Between 1992 and 1998 Marc ran a successful home brew business in Bridgend. The shop was not just a place to buy from but also a place for customers to speak to fellow brewers and wine makers with coffee freely thrown in.

Not content with just selling kits and ingredients Marc constantly brewed both wine and beer on the premises so that customers could see how the processes worked and to taste the final results.

Marc let customer demand decide where to buy his stock from and this led to dealings with Tuckers Maltings and Brupaks in the quest for quality ingredients for his customers. His ethos was you can only make quality beer with quality ingredients. It was an ethos that served him and his customers well.

Sadly the homebrew shop in Bridgend closed in April 1998, after 6 fantastic years, and Marc eventually moved from Wales to Norfolk, where he now enjoys the Norfolk Broads and works for a large public sector employer.